# CHOOSING TO
# LEAD

Joy —
Thanks for all you
have done !!

# HARVEY KANTER

# CHOOSING TO LEAD

## Being Comfortable
## Being Uncomfortable

FOREWORD BY SHARON DALOZ PARKS

# CHOOSING TO LEAD

Being Comfortable Being Uncomfortable

ISBN (print): 978-1-7333517-1-3
ISBN (kindle): 978-1-7333517-0-6
Library of Congress Control Number: 2019910510

Cover Design: Mark Albert
Writing and creative partner: Wendy K. Walters

To contact the author: info@harveykanter.com

**HARVEYKANTER.COM**

TO MOM AND DAD

You placed in me the core values which
have become my life's road map.

TO MY WIFE, ROBIN

You have always been by my side.
Without your support, it is hard to imagine
all this could ever have happened!

# PRAISE FOR CHOOSING TO LEAD

Having worked alongside Harvey in the past, I found his book to be not only a reflection of his leadership style; authentic, transparent and values based, but a powerful lens into the application and impact of true leadership. I applaud Harvey for being comfortable being uncomfortable!

—BRIAN CORNELL
CEO, TARGET

Harvey's quest for meaning creates a touching, inspiring, and humbling masterpiece. *Choosing to Lead* is not just another book about leadership. It is a thoughtful and useful reflection on the power of curiosity, unconventional thinking, teamwork and the value of inspiring others. A must read!

—FREDERIC CUMENAL
FORMER CEO OF TIFFANY & CO.
FORMER CEO & PRESIDENT OF CHAMPAGNE MOËT & CHANDON SCS

I was inspired by Harvey Kanter's book, *Choosing to Lead,* because it represents an honest, insightful and transparent reflection of a thoughtful leader's personal journey. Harvey reminds us that the most influential leaders create meaningful and sustainable impact on the lives they touch as well as the businesses they empower. This, in turn, can create a wonderful cascading effect throughout companies and careers.

—TIERNEY B. REMICK
VICE CHAIR BOARD AND CEO PRACTICE, KORN FERRY INTERNATIONAL

In *Choosing to Lead*, Harvey emphasizes that humble leaders create and drive a culture around a desire to learn and explore. This inspires others to push, to take risks, to step up, and to step out. This book offers sound and practical advice for leading organizations. It is a smart reading for any executive who aspires to be a great leader.

—DAVID HUMPHREY
**MANAGING DIRECTOR, BAIN CAPITAL PARTNERS, LP**

*Choosing to Lead* is a quintessential leadership book—significantly impactful! The read of Harvey's journey is a must, the lessons learned and his real-life examples are applicable, practical, and relevant to any person who wants to lead successfully, execute wisely, and strategize innovatively.

—LORIANN V. LOWERY-BIGGERS
**CEO, BELLAVAUGHAN, INC.**
**CORPORATE BOARD DIRECTOR, FORMER PRESIDENT OF NORTH AMERICA, LLOYD'S OF LONDON, INC.**

Harvey Kanter's career provides a treasure trove of easily relatable yet highly impactful leadership lessons. He has "been there and done that" and brilliantly illustrates many real-world examples as actionable lessons whereby every reader can extract real impact.

—DAN LEVITAN
**CO-FOUNDER & PARTNER, MAVERON**

*Choosing to Lead* is such a powerful reminder of quiet confidence and how it can be portrayed in inspiring ways. In all my 40 years in retail and being exposed to many leaders, never once did arrogance motivate me. Quiet confidence, on the other hand, seen through remarkable leadership for and about the team stood above all else in creating a culture. That quiet confidence was like a magnet ever pulling the team forward.

—MINDY MEADS
**40-YEAR RETAIL VETERAN
FORMER CEO LANDS END,
FORMER CEO VICTORIA'S SECRET DIRECT, FORMER CO-CEO AEROPOSTALE**

Service to others is the rent you pay for your room here on earth.

**MUHAMMAD ALI**

# CONTENTS

# Foreword by Sharon Daloz Parks

The phrase, "the art and practice of leadership" has long been in use. Only in recent years have we begun to take in what it means. Our notions of leadership, our deep and powerful myths about what it means to lead, our default settings when we think about what leading an organization, community, or nation requires, have been rooted in images of lone heroes in command, leading the charge.

These great myths are now under review. We find ourselves asked to live at one of those great hinge points in history, a time of profound disruption and change, spawning unprecedented challenges—environmental, technological, social-economic-political, moral, spiritual. Our cultural assumptions are being upended in the face of environmental consciousness, globalization, and the intensification of complexity, and it is in this context that we are undergoing a reconsideration of what we mean by "leadership." Lone heroes are having a harder time winning the day. In today's world, there is a hunger and a call for "adaptive-creative leadership" that can help organizations move from familiar patterns that are no longer fitting, through the rapids of change, to create new patterns more fitting to what is now required. The key word is "create."

To create is to bring into form what has not existed before. We have regarded "creativity" as something "artists"—the creative types—do, and we have recognized that art and artistry require imagination. But in the rough and tumble of the business sector, "creativity" has typically been consigned to the margins, presuming that the "real work" of leadership primarily requires the capacity to wield power, make tough decisions, and act decisively. Leadership does, indeed, require the capacity to navigate the currents of power, to make significant decisions, and to act with confidence. But in this hinge time, we are discovering that we have a great deal to learn about additional and essential qualities of leadership from those we conventionally recognize as artists.

Artists know that creativity requires wading into and staying with what feels conflicted, out of whack, dissonant, and sometimes overwhelming—moving into rather than denying or merely "fixing" the challenge at hand. Artists know also that the process sometimes requires pausing, waiting, listening, observing, taking time for the mud to settle. Artists know how to stay centered on the edge where the familiar patterns can give way to emerging possibilities. And artists learn how to shed what is no longer viable as they prototype—that is, run experiments—knowing that both the successes and the failures will cast light leading to the best outcome. And like any great potter, artist-leaders in today's world know that they must bring their best work to the test of the fire—whether it be the fire of the board room or the C-suite, the press or the labor union, the shareholders or the neighborhood.

Great leaders in today's world also submit their endeavors to the test of their conscience and the life of the commons. They seek to align their work with their own moral compass, while working the question of what will optimally serve the common good. Knowing that everything is connected to everything else, their field of action and deepest purposes both include and transcend the bottom line of their own organization.

The artistry of leadership today is less like that of a painter alone in the attic and much more like the conductor of an orchestra, the director in the theatre, or the jazz pianist. Each continually works with an ensemble of others and hands off essential features of the creative, building process—to colleagues, engineers, accountants, the sales force, human resource managers, suppliers, department heads—inspiring each of them to bring their own artistry to the work. Indeed, a fact at the core of adaptive-creative leadership is that *you don't even think of doing it alone*—no one can move a complex system by themselves.

Like all artistry, learning adaptive-creative leadership requires honing a set of skills, becoming competent in the craft, repeatedly risking failure, learning a discipline of soul—allowing one's self to be changed over time. This kind of learning and becoming requires practice, practice, practice. As one watercolor painter has put it, "It requires many miles on the brush."

Great painters are steeped in learning from continuous practice—and they don't just hang out alone in the attic. They learn, in part, by looking over the shoulder of other painters—in the studio, at the edge of a landscape, or in a gallery or museum. They study and watch each other practice. Then they return to their own practice and reach beyond where others have gone—gifting us with their distinctive contribution.

Harvey Kanter is generously inviting us to observe his more than forty years of practice—to look over his shoulder and through his mind, heart, and hand. In this book, *Choosing to Lead,* Kanter reveals his own journey in the adventure of learning the artistry of leadership as a businessman and as a citizen of the commons. He offers a compelling example of how curiosity, tenacity, teamwork and shared accomplishment, dialogue, values, decisiveness, and optimism in the face of setbacks play in the alchemy of effective leadership. In this time of both peril and promise when we hunger for masterful leadership, he provides a lens through which we each can gain vital and meaningful insight into "the art and practice of leadership."

—SHARON DALOZ PARKS

AUTHOR, *LEADERSHIP CAN BE TAUGHT*
DISTINGUISHED FACULTY, EXECUTIVE LEADERSHIP PROGRAM, SEATTLE UNIVERSITY

If we are to truly expand
and develop our leadership
perspective, we must first get
outside our own minds and
"think about our thinking."

**RONALD A. HEIFETZ**
(Paraphrased)

Introduction

# THE LENS THROUGH WHICH TO LOOK

"Average leaders raise the bar on themselves;
good leaders raise the bar for others;
great leaders inspire others to raise their own bar."

**ORRIN WOODWARD**
Founder & Chairman of the Board of Life,

New York Times Best Selling Author

The function of a leader is to guide and counsel, to instill confidence and enthusiasm, to create momentum and inspiration for others in their desire to be the best they can be. But leadership is about so much more than this. The way you live your life, the choices you make, how you take risks and embrace responsibility, the way in which you own outcomes are all part of the unique recipe for the kind of leader you will be. Beyond just the way in which you do things, leadership is about who you are.

I was born driven. I began by running my own business detailing cars when I was sixteen and by the time I was eighteen, I had bought and sold twenty-one cars. A few weeks into college I found a girlfriend and  two weeks after graduation, we were married. During college I had an internship working for Target® Stores which helped set up my early career in retail where I spent eight years with Carter Hawley Hale (serving in eight different roles). I went on to work for two years with Sears® in their pursuit to become a national department store. From there I enjoyed eight years in senior leadership with Eddie Bauer®. While there, I had the great fortune to be asked to participate in a wonderful experience created by Seattle University's Center for Leadership in their Graduate Program of studies.

That led to the opportunity to serve as President of Aaron Brothers® Art & Framing for three years, followed by three more years as the Executive Vice President and Chief Merchandising Officer serving the world's largest craft retailer, Michaels. After that I joined Moosejaw Mountaineering and Backcountry Travel as the CEO for a little over three years before accepting the baton to serve as CEO of Blue Nile®, the world's largest online diamond retailer. In 2019, I transitioned to the role of CEO and president of Destination XL Group (DXL Group). With more than 325 stores, they are the largest specialty retailer of men's XL apparel. I continue to serve as Chairman of the Board for Blue Nile® and sit on the boards of several companies and charitable organizations.

I share this "resume" simply to be upfront and open about what I have done in my career. It is the background from which I have gained insights on the subject of leadership. I am not my resume. These roles do not define my character, my integrity, or my personality. I am more than my resume, but in the context of a book on leadership, leadership experience is relevant. It is from this body of experience and the journey through each season of my life that I share with you what I have been privileged to learn along the way.

Though I never set out to be a "leader," I have become one. While the case can be made that in my DNA there is buried some innate leadership qualities, there is no question in my mind that circumstances, opportunities, and mentors have worked together to shape these skills. Whatever was already present in my nature has been further nurtured by these things, developed and enhanced until the word "leader" is as accurate a description of me as the words "husband" or "father" or "man". Mentors have played a critical role in my development, and I look forward to introducing mine to you.

Written not as a memoir or biography, but rather as a collection of thoughts and experiences, *Choosing to Lead* is the journaled expedition of my life's pursuit to lead and create meaning. It is not meant to be a "How To" book for you to follow, but more a reflection of "How I Have" and the insights I gained along the way. I trust you will apply them as you see fit. In my constant dedication to improvement, I have enjoyed the rich benefits of that personal development in my career, in my marriage and family life, through meaningful relationships, and in serving my community. My writing chronicles areas which I have explored and what I learned, then have attempted to practice and hone. It is my hope these will prove valuable to you in your own pursuit of becoming the best leader you can be.

In my pursuit, I find that my actions are a continuous expression of my values—my moral compass—and my desire to make a positive impact. I want to make a difference, not just be a person passing through life. If in sharing my story, your own ability to become a better person, make a difference, and leave a lasting, positive impact is improved, then I will have met my goal for writing this book. As we begin, it seems relevant to share a little about how I grew up and introduce you to my first mentors.

# A BIT OF BACKGROUND

I had the privilege of growing up in a warm, loving family. My mother and father had three children, giving me one older sister and one younger—leaving me smack in the middle. We were from the East Coast, more specifically the Northeast, with my parents being from New Jersey and Connecticut (more or less). My dad was sixteen and my mom just fourteen when they first met. They married a few years later and had fifty great years together before my mom died peacefully at a young seventy years of age. Through the natural engagement of parent and child, they taught me commitment, communication, and the value of family. My dad (knock on wood) is now eighty-three and has found love for the second time. And although this relationship is much different than the one he had with my mother, it's all good! My bedrock was formed by the way my parents lived their life together—their steadfastness, faithfulness, and tenacity are the foundational elements of all things good in my life.

Though we started out on the East Coast we moved several times, eventually ending up in the Midwest with its "salt of the earth" people, and the small town charm which provided a great place to grow up. Eager to explore what this great country had to offer, we traveled all over by car and by plane. We would pile into the family sedan and drive to the Upper Peninsula, then on to Door County, Wisconsin. I can still feel how smooth and cool the rocks were in my hand, polished by the constant tumbling and washing of the waves of Lake Superior. I tried to skip those rocks, but it was also fun to throw them as far I could, or watch them plunk into the water to see how big a splash they could make. Later we would picnic by the water, enjoying the sound of the waves lapping on the shore, the breeze off the lake sending our napkins sailing.

We drove to the Badlands of North Dakota and I marveled at the fabulous shapes made by the clay-rich soil, eroded by wind and water. We saw the massively carved faces in Mt. Rushmore and visited the Crazy Horse Memorial where we camped out in pop-up trailers. We flew to Disneyland and did the park. We explored. We laughed, and in general, were exposed to all life has to offer. Mostly, we had great fun.

My mother was a typical mom of the times—definitely old-school. She created a household and family life that was supportive of my father and his pursuits in business. My mom had once worked, but eventually evolved into the traditional role of many stay-at-home moms in the sixties. She made sure we had a hot, cooked breakfast every morning and wonderful family meals at night. More often than not, and because the food was always abundant and delicious, my friends also found their way around our table for meals.

It was a wonderful environment in which to grow up: rich in values, mixed with a little bit of religious upbringing, and discipline typical of the times. My family life was warm and supportive and this impacted me as much then as it does now in raising my own family or leading an organization.

My father was a retailer, and a multi-generational one at that. My father's father was a tailor and his mom took care of the books.

My mother's father owned a large furniture business in Danbury, Connecticut, and the generations before them were also retailers. It was what we did, so it was natural for me to take the baton from my father and become a retailer as well.

Whatever elements make up my DNA, this rich family life and the way I was brought up has created in me a desire to make a lasting difference. My experiences, along with the people who have made up the cast of characters surrounding me, have molded and shaped me into the man I am today. That man is evolving still.

## LET THE GAMES BEGIN

This is not a paint-by-number leadership guide or an offer of some proven formula for success. However, if you have curiosity in your soul, if you are prone to wonder about things, if you want to be more and do more and lead better, then my musings may just help you leverage your own experiences and spark new growth in you as a leader.

In pages to come, we'll explore a few of the elements I have found to be most valuable in leadership. We'll begin with a discussion of what leadership really means and address the importance of communication, the role of optimism, and handling setbacks. We'll spend time discussing values—not so much individual values (honor, respect, positivity, etc.), but the bedrock for how core tenets frame the life of a leader and impact the way in which they lead.

I'll share a transformational experience that completely re-framed my values and forever shifted the landscape of leadership for me. That experience changed my definition of accomplishment and forever altered my perspective. It created a new metric to help me lead people to become the best they could be—not my definition of the best, but theirs. It shifted my perspective of winning and I hope it will challenge you as well.

We will talk about curiosity and the value of developing a life-long orientation to learning. We'll visit about humility and confidence and the roles these play in today's morally challenging, complex climate. We will talk about the key role tenacity and perseverance play in ones' ability to lead well and find success. We'll address diversity and how a leader encourages dialogue, nurtures debate, and navigates different points of view to connect the intellect and experiences of others, mining their insights and fostering a culture of innovative thought.

I'll share one of my favorite aspects of leadership; adventure. Engaging in adventurous activities helps a leader create the agility to become a catalyst for change, stimulates subconscious problem-solving, and forces leaders to see things from a new point of view. Adventure expands your capacity for resilience and builds confidence to navigate unknown territory. From there we'll connect the dots from adventure to action and how this informs the ability to make and execute decisions. Action-oriented leaders create action-oriented teams, so we'll talk about how to make decisions under less-than-ideal circumstances and when faced with unknown factors in the presence of pressures for performance and time.

We'll pull all those elements together and discuss teamwork; how collaborative leadership encourages team members to contribute ideas and strategy, ultimately crafting the path others will follow to reach a common goal or destination. We'll explore insights into how a good leader facilitates the talents and abilities of each member of their team and leverages them for successful outcomes—how to get the best out of the people for which you are accountable to lead.

Finally, no examination of leadership would be complete without considering legacy. For me, my legacy as a leader is centered around making a difference and impacting people in a positive and lasting way. But it isn't about my legacy or even about how to create your legacy. Consideration of the legacy you wish to create forces you to understand your motivation for being a leader. I hope to inspire you to think about what it is you want to accomplish and how you will go about doing that. I want you to have greater clarity regarding your own definition of achievement and explore which avenues to pursue, which lens to look through, and what thought process to engage with that will make sure you accomplish whatever it is you have set out to do.

I promise to share my experiences transparently and present a road map of leadership territory and the course I have charted through it. Which route you choose to follow and how you tease these elements out and apply them to your life is up to you. I invite you to engage with me through the pages of this book and thoughtfully consider the possibilities afforded through the intentional development of your leadership capacity.

# Chapter One

# LEADERSHIP
## WHAT DOES IT REALLY MEAN

"The greatest leader is not necessarily the one who does the greatest things. He is the one that gets the people to do the greatest things."

**RONALD REAGAN**
Former U.S. President

L eaders lead. Regardless of position, title, or level of authority, when you inspire and empower others to pursue work together as a team, you are a leader.

Broken down to its simplest function, leaders set a course for others to follow. Leaders help to define what can be done together as a team. Collaborative leadership encourages members to contribute ideas and strategy, ultimately crafting the path to follow to reach a common goal or destination. Leaders set the course and then facilitate following this course by offering support for what that is going to look like and how the team is going to get there. **A leader is there to guide and counsel, to instill confidence and enthusiasm, to create momentum and**

**inspiration for others in their desire to be the best they can be.** In short, leaders empower people.

This empowerment permits all involved to march to a shared destination together in unison. When identifying a leader, there are three components I look for:

- Their actions—What is it they actually do?

- Their words—Is there congruency between what they say and what they do?

- The environment they create—Do they know when to lead and when to follow, when to sit back and watch? Do they understand the dynamics of the team? Do they serve and support a culture of respect, collaboration, and creativity?

Having people look to you for guidance can be very affirming. Sometimes they will see you in your element, operating with confidence in the best of circumstances. However, they don't just look to you, they also look at you. At times they will see you leading them and forging ahead in uncharted waters, learning to navigate as you go. This is a great example of the "cutting edge" as a leader leads into the unexplored, with the risks inherent in the unknown. Leading invites opportunities to be seen in both the best light possible where the path is well worn, as well as from a less than comfortable vantage point where the path is unfamiliar, and the outcome unknown and ambiguous.

I attended Arizona State University (ASU) for my undergraduate work. A large school, this was and remains a great institution which is respected for both its progressiveness and innovative curriculum. While I was studying there, more than 60,000 students were in attendance. This meant undergraduate class sizes could be quite large. Lectures for an underclassman in courses like Marketing 101 or Financing 101 were presented "auditorium style," with students seated the full width of the hall and as many as fifty rows deep. While I was never a front row kind of a guy, I could usually be seen seated somewhere towards the front of the class. The setting did not naturally lend itself to a lively discussion, so at times students would gather around the professor at the end of class to ask questions. The trouble was that the lecture ran 50 minutes long and the break between classes was only ten minutes long.

You probably already recognize that Arizona is hot. Really hot. Sprinting from one class to another in the 100° heat did not appeal to me, nor did being late to my next class. On top of that, I didn't want to forget my questions or have them pile up. So, rather than try to catch the professor during the in-between, I would just raise my hand and ask my question when it came to mind.

My girlfriend (now wife) would say things like, "I can't believe you just did that, asked that!" or "Why didn't you wait until the end of class?" She would never have raised her hand, never have wanted to call all that attention to herself like that.

Fortunately, the teacher liked interaction in the class. And for me, not only was I not grandstanding, I would get this warm, uncomfortable feeling as I raised my hand, wondering if people thought I was an idiot for asking or for admitting I didn't understand something just presented. I didn't like people staring at me then any more than I do now. But, I needed clarification. If I needed to know something, I would ask.

Invariably, some student would catch me on the way out the door and say something like, "Hey, that was a great question ... I really wanted to know too, but I didn't want to ask." This small act of raising my hand to ask a question in a room filled with 500 students was at some level, risk-taking. Was I asking a good question? Did others have the same question? One of my favorite sayings now is, "Be comfortable being uncomfortable." Back then I most certainly was not.

That said, I was willing to step into the vacuum and so began what you might say is a life of being comfortable with being uncomfortable. Whenever there was some element that wasn't clear to me, I could either live in a black hole and not know (hoping it might become clear by some other means), or just ask a question. Raising my hand to ask a question was something I could do, it just seemed appropriate. More than that, it was something I should do because it needed to be done—not just for my benefit, but also because it might provide greater insight to those around me as well. From the responses of my girlfriend and others, it was clear they were uneasy about stepping into that vacuum, unwilling to go down an unfamiliar path. Intended or not, I was leading.

# THE ABILENE PARADOX[1]

One hot July afternoon, a young couple was visiting their parents in Coleman, Texas. The father-in-law suddenly suggested they all hop in the car and take a trip to Abilene to get dinner. The daughter agreed, "Sounds like a great idea ..." Because his wife agreed, the young man also gave his approval to the plan, followed by the mother-in-law. They all took the 53-mile drive to Abilene in their unairconditioned '58 Buick. The trip was miserable. When they got back, through a quick exchange they each learned that none of them had wanted to go in the first place. The suggestion had been made casually and all had given their agreement to the plan, but no one knew why they had gone in the first place. None had enjoyed the journey. No one questioned the motivation or the destination. Preferring not to challenge the idea or upset the status quo, each participated unwillingly, inherently knowing it was a bad plan from the beginning.

Leaders must be willing to put themselves into uncomfortable, vulnerable positions—be comfortable being uncomfortable. They must obtain clarity to chart a course to a destination that makes sense. The bad-case scenario in asking questions is that someone chuckles at you while you learn. The worse-case scenario is you drive 53 miles in the Texas heat with no air conditioning, and have a lousy meal as your reward. Conversely, the best-case scenario results in you or your team being able to take thoughtful, relevant action because you learned something worthwhile.

You do not need to have all the answers to be a leader, but you do have to be willing to figure them out if you are going to chart a path clear enough for others to follow. And ... you are going to make some mistakes. People rise to certain levels in an organization: associates, specialists, supervisors, managers, senior managers, executives (and so forth) within the context of many variables. Often enough, skills can be learned, and while many say leadership is a product of nature, it can be nurtured too. Along the way there will be challenges, risks, and at times failure. Those who are not humble enough to accept failure will be unable to rise. Leaders must have the will and the skill to allow themselves to become successful as they grow in the complexity of their role and embrace the increasing responsibilities of those roles. Leaders will keep seeking answers until they find them.

**YOU DO NOT NEED TO HAVE ALL THE ANSWERS TO BE A LEADER, BUT YOU DO NEED TO BE WILLING TO FIGURE THEM OUT**

More times than I can recount, I have experienced that same warm, uncomfortable feeling I had when asking questions back in Marketing 101 ... maybe no one understands, I know I don't. Sometimes you don't know if the decision you are making is the right decision or not. It could be the wrong one, but if no one makes the decision, then what? Will you just let the cards fall where they may? If no one makes a decision, then where do you go? You might end up in Abilene, hot, miserable and confused. If you are the one who put everyone in the car, then you are responsible for dragging them there. Once you have made a decision, you are accountable for the outcomes. If you have assessed the risk and reward (and if it is not life-or-death) and you make the wrong decision, you simply live and learn.

Many say intuition is just years of experience, not really a whole lot more. There are many great reasons to ask questions and making the best decision possible with the information available is one of them, but it can't happen if you don't ask. Even if asking is uncomfortable and you are uneasy in doing so, asking questions is paramount to leading well.

We are going to cover many elements of leadership in chapters to come, but here in the context of defining what leadership is, there are a few fundamentals which need to be addressed.

## COMMUNICATION

Communication is the single most important element in leadership, bar none. Possessing the ability to create leverage and have people know what the rallying cry is, having the ability to be efficient and effective at outcomes, being able to recognize and define what success looks like are all the result of great communication.

Even when everyone is in agreement about the destination—where they want to go and what lies at the end of the road—they still have all kinds of ideas about how to get there. To chart a clear course people are willing to follow, I practice these three things:

- **Look**: I look for touch points where there is a preponderance of people wanting to do things a certain way. I pay attention to these, they are relevant markers to heed.

- **Listen**: I listen to the team, genuinely attentive to why they believe one way is better than another, and I invite feedback.

- **Learn**: I pay attention to why some ideas did or did not work historically. This allows me to connect the dots and see the bigger picture.

Two-way communication is vital. Once information is taken in (looked at, listened to, learned from) the next step is to play this back to members of the team and say, "Here's what I heard and absorbed. Here's what you told me, and this is my perspective on what that means." This allows for meaningful exchange. It helps build consensus and allows the leader to say, "Here is the path we should go down and here's why." This may be followed by another round of two-way communication, but the result is that a strategy is created, informed by a vision. Leaders who look, listen, and learn are able to establish and communicate what markers will be important and how the team will measure reaching them along the way.

Dialogue informs your view while sharing others' views and the path you are charting is either affirmed or created as a result. From this collaboration, the leader can define and inform the strategy. Decisions are more sure-footed and well-received because of the collaborative process. Let's consider the alternative.

## LEADERSHIP STYLE

On the opposite end of the scale is another approach to leadership which is dictatorial in orientation and primarily exercises one-way communication. As an example of this, imagine a fear-based culture where the leader essentially tells the team: "Here is where we are going. Here is how we are going to get there. Execute it perfectly or else." Whenever the plan does not work out as expected, the team's experience will be to duck for cover in order not to get taken out. Punitive ramifications often take place.

Make no mistake, the company can still be a meaningful entity and even experience notable financial success. But this kind of leadership will eventually run out of runway, lose its perspective, and misplace the roadmap. There will be an endpoint at which to arrive rather than a vision from which to evolve.

This dictatorial approach is not inspiring. It is punitive rather than fulfilling. This kind of non-collaborative environment run by one-way communication is fine as long as everything is working, but when something goes wrong (and something will eventually always go wrong) someone is sure to be on the chopping block. As a result, turnover will be high and satisfaction low. People will not be engaged with the vision or the brand, only with compensation, and when this runs its course, turnover will be greatly accelerated.

I have experienced this leadership style on more than one occasion at more than one organization. In one such situation I was given license to address and adjust the culture to bring about a shift. In response, I interviewed a hundred people and took hundreds of pages of notes, listening to each person in order to learn. I was a like a detective on assignment—uncovering why they were there and where they hoped to go next, discovering what each person was now engaged in that they weren't before. I invited feedback, encouraged dialogue, welcomed creativity and fresh perspective and was able to create a new path from their input. We changed up what they had been doing, modified the strategy and tactics. While doing that, we also worked on "the us"— our culture. As a result, sales increased, motivation and commitment returned, and the rate of turnover declined by over 40% in the first twelve months. The team responded favorably to the collaborative style of leadership and the tangible results were undeniable.

## VISION AND STRATEGY

The leader needs a long-term view. Strategy plays with the long game in mind, and casting vision is a leader's job. Costco Founder James Sinegal says, "I think the biggest single thing that causes difficulty in the business world is the short-term view. We become obsessed with it, but it forces bad decisions." Vision formed through a long-range lens and involving a collaborative process will result in better decisions being made. Ultimately, the leader is responsible for articulating and defining the vision—what it is we want to accomplish. Once clear, the strategy is "How do we do this?"

For example, say your business is car rentals—old-school I know, and a rapidly changing industry, but bear with me. A car rental business provides a framework to illustrate a foundational concept surrounding the complexity of creating a vision and strategy (or the lack thereof). We will not look at the business through the eyes of the evolving consumer, but rather, let's take a moment and put ourselves in the position of owning a rental car business. Let's say you have a clear vision to be the best car rental company in the United States. You first have to define what "the best" means and from there can decide the best brands of the cars as determined by which are the most highly desirable to consumers (as defined by your vision of best). To strategically support the vision, you would also need to determine additional elements of what "best" means. For example, you would need to negotiate the ability to create the greatest value for those cars, defining what convenience looks like, what are the vehicle features, pickup and return ease, etc. Strategy maps out the course for how the vision will be reached.

## TACTICS AND OPERATING

With a clear vision (what we want to accomplish) and strategy (how we want to accomplish this), the leader would continue to collaborate with the team. In turn the team's leaders would, by working with their teams, determine the operations and logistics required to execute the strategy. In our car rental example, things which must be determined are elements such as: How do we keep the cars filled with gas? How do we keep them clean? How do we keep them from breaking down? These are the tactics for running the business. A leader will exhaust themselves and limit the capacity for growth and the potential of their team unless they empower other people to determine, based on their own leadership abilities, how to accomplish the work. The leader is accountable to provide the broad context and establish basic parameters, then those further down determine the details and create tangible operating plans to support the vision.

Let's say you are in Seattle and want to get to New York City. Getting to New York is the vision, but beyond the decision that we are driving to get there, there are many routes which could be taken to reach the desired destination. Do we go through Montana, South Dakota, Minnesota ... or do we choose to go down south towards Nevada, head through Arizona, New Mexico, Texas, Arkansas, and Tennessee? As the leader, you empower your team to know how to get there on their own.

Vision alone is not enough. The team needs some other parameters such as the purpose of getting to New York. Is it a tourist expedition or a trucking route? What is the time frame in which they need to arrive? The operating budget? This information allows the team to determine the tactics. Say it is a trucking route, then in winter when snow and ice could delay shipping, a southern route makes more sense. Plotting as much freeway as possible increases efficiency. But say it is for vacation and tourism. Then by all means go old school and travel the rambling two-lane Route 66! Stop at great diners and scenic overlooks and buy little refrigerator magnets from every state as you pass. The key is once vision is clear and strategy is known, allow the people closest to the situation to determine the best way to get it done.

# DECISION MAKING

Many people have trouble making decisions. The same can be said of organizations in totality, and stemming from their leadership. Making a decision inherently involves risk. As an individual, even picking a restaurant stresses some people out. When you come to a fork in the road, have to pick right or left. You often do not know what the right path is. If you take the wrong fork, you could end up somewhere you don't want to go. But the choice is yours alone: do you stand still or deal with the outcomes? Making decisions is an inherent requirement of an effective leader, and accepting responsibility for the results goes hand in hand.

Picture a leader who has some staff above them, and a larger staff below. This person, while not at the top of the pyramid, is somewhere well above the mid-line, and as such is required to make decisions, many decisions. Those who work under them also make lots of decisions. This leader is accountable to those above not only for every decision they make, but also for every decision made by those who work below them. It would be impossible for them to make (or even approve) every decision necessary if the operation is to keep flowing smoothly. Ultimately, as the "leader," this individual is accountable.

Though not making every decision, they are responsible for the outcomes of the team. Therefore, it is in their best interest to embrace process, structure, and discipline. They will not be content to just send a strategy memo and hope for the best, but instead will want to create metrics to assess success, be able to course correct, and deliver on objectives. An effective leader should have no problem making decisions.

## ACTION

Have you ever worked in an environment where people do not act until they are told to do so? What motivates you to act? How do you function in environments where the work is largely undefined? Can you juggle variables and respond to ever-changing conditions? Do others set their pace by you? Is there a fire in your belly?

Leadership happens when there is something that needs to be defined: strategy, organizational structure, outcomes expected, etc. These things need to be made clear by somebody and as the leader, you are now accountable for those definitions. You have to act without being told what to do or how to do it. High-level leaders are extremely vulnerable because their actions are on display, the stakes are high. Consequences are broad and visible. This for certain can be high risk and can equate to a high reward as well. That said, leaders don't take action for the reward, leaders act because they are in (or have been put into) a position requiring something needing definition. Anointed as a leader or not and regardless of title, stepping in to define what is unclear so others can see, agree, and act together makes you a leader.

Now consider the work environment of a server in a fast-casual restaurant or an Uber driver. In these situations, the job is well-defined. Personality determines if they will be friendly and accurate and efficient, but a lot of the thinking has been done for them. They don't have to lead in the definitional essence of leadership. There is a checklist to follow which someone else has mapped out for them. For the driver, an app tells them where the customer is located, calculates the best route to follow, computes the fare (even suggests the tip), helps them avoid traffic— all given to the driver so they don't have to think about logistics, just execute. They have decidedly less risk than a manager would, let alone the CEO of a company, and therefore, less reward.

A leader willing to act fosters action in their team. Actions speak louder than words. I know, this is a cliché, but it became one for a good reason. Action from a leader sets the pace for the whole team. It establishes the tone and creates the expectation. Their actions can support or further establish the culture and way of doing things. Equally, when a leader is seen "doing what needs to be done," a precedent is established for the team that you need to jump in and take action, not wait for someone else to act. It supports and defines their leadership by their actions, not their words.

# INSPIRATION

Those who authentically enjoy who they are and what they do inspire those around them. Passion expressed has an infectious energy. Self-motivated leaders who champion small wins and function from genuinely-held beliefs create energy in their team. Inspiration has the greatest capacity to motivate others and rally them around an initiative.

You never hire people to fail, but by allowing them the freedom to try things (with the chance things may go wrong) you unleash them to explore roles that open up new and unexpected possibilities. People enjoy working with and for leaders who are not only willing to allow them to take risks, but encourage them to make decisions, collaborate, understand and accept risk, and grow in their capacity to lead. Being part of an inspirational culture has deep, intrinsic value and attracts bright, creative, motivated people—the kind of people good leaders want to be part of their team.

# CULTURE

Families and organizations all have a culture, an environment surrounding them created by what is important to them, what inspires them, how they communicate with each other, their shared passions, shared accomplishments, and shared history. The culture affects how members interact with one another, whether positively or negatively. In my life, I strive to be genuine, direct, transparent, and straightforward. I am not punitive, I speak with respect, and respond from a place of commitment. As a leader I have the capacity to define the culture of my organization, and every day when I get up and as I go about my day, I have the opportunity to do and be this person.

If I don't operate in and support the culture of my choosing, then the environment will shape itself without my influence. It is easy to communicate and say you (and your organization) have a culture of respect, perseverance in adversity, fortitude, optimism … until something goes horribly wrong and you and your team are challenged to function within the parameters of the culture you have established. In those moments, the responses and actions of you and your team will either uphold and strengthen the fabric of the culture, or tear it apart thread by thread. You own yourself, and you have the opportunity to mold, hold accountable, inspect, and expect the same within your team.

Earlier I mentioned a company where dictatorial leadership had created an unhealthy, fear-based culture. The company's culture was broken. To fix it, we first needed to learn what was driving the high turnover and listen to the concerns and expectations of staff. After much two-way conversation and when a good barometer of what was and wasn't important had been established, I called a town hall meeting bringing the entire company together. It was time to shift the culture. I stood up in front of the company and communicated: "Here's what I heard, and here's where we are headed. This is who we are, and this is who we are going to become. If you're on board this will be a great place to work. If you don't like these terms, then the door is right there." This was the first step to fostering a new culture. It would take time, but a new ethos began to emerge.

Research Fortune's list of 100 Best Companies to Work For® and you will soon learn these organizations have half the voluntary turnover rate as their industry peers. Why is this? What sort of work environments have they been able to successfully create and sustain?

It doesn't take too deep a probe to discover that people want to be meaningfully connected to the purpose of the company they work for, not just punch a clock. It is no shock to learn that people prefer a high trust culture where they feel empowered to do their job and rewarded for taking risks and being creative. People genuinely enjoy being part of a community, value having their contributions recognized, and appreciate being treated with respect and given a voice. Regardless of how great individuals within an organization may be, this kind of healthy cultural environment does not happen without focused intention and deliberate, diligent nurture.

Culture can be defined across variables as broad in scope as ethics and core values. It encompasses things like positivity, respectfulness, authenticity, curiosity, tenacity, how a team responds to challenges and adversity, solves problems, resolves conflict, how they handle mistakes … and the list goes on. A company's culture is the bedrock of its foundation. Commitment to the defined culture is a key indicator for the way work gets done and how goals get met.

Without a tangible and profound depth in commitment to these cultural principles, an environment of fear, punishment, and mistrust will cause an organization to shrivel at its core. A team's inspired commitment can't be bought, but its authentic being is priceless and the culture that drives it is irreplaceable for driving results.

## PUTTING IT ALL TOGETHER

If we were to put all these things under one giant leadership umbrella: communication, style, vision and strategy, tactics and operating, decision making, taking action, inspiration, and the culture created, how then do we define the function of a leader? With so many facets of leadership being examined, the job description of "leader" seems almost too over-arching to be tangibly practical.

For me, **the function of a leader is to guide and counsel, to instill confidence and enthusiasm, to create momentum and inspiration for others in their desire to be the best they can be.** The leader must define, communicate, and lead by example those values that are espoused to be the standard for behavior. What the organization stands for and how this is demonstrated each and every day is set by the leader through the actions and expectations that leader delivers. Teammates are inspired to be the best they can be, are held accountable to the standard, and this thriving, wholesome culture allows the organization and the individuals in it to prosper.

As you read and digest this, there are some questions to consider with regards to how you view your role and pinpoint areas in which you can grow as a leader:

- Is it a role in which you can provide guidance and counsel?

- Do you instill confidence and enthusiasm in others?

- Do your actions create momentum and inspiration for others in their desire to be the best they can be?

- Or, at a minimum, do you see yourself working in an organization and/or for a leader who is doing these things?

- Do you find yourself inspired?

- Do you see a path to creating a bigger impact and is that a path where you see yourself?

- As you define leadership and what makes sense for who you are, are you comfortable being uncomfortable?

Before we dive into specific elements of leadership, I want to share a personal story with you about a time when I encountered a devastating obstacle. The leader I had become before this life event gave me a deep well from which to draw and served me by having developed great resilience. So as we begin our leadership journey together, let's start with what it looks like to face a setback.

## ENDNOTE

1. Harvey, Jerry B. *The Abilene Paradox and Other Meditations on Management.* Jossey-Bass. 1988.

Chapter Two

# SETBACKS
## WE FOUND A SMALL TUMOR ... WE THINK IT'S JUST A FATTY TISSUE (A.K.A. DON'T WORRY)

"The ability to bounce back after a setback is the single most important trait an entrepreneur can possess."

**RICHARD BRANSON**
Business Magnate, Founder of the Virgin Group

At one point in my career, I had the great privilege to serve as President of Aaron Brothers Art and Framing which allowed me the experience of becoming part of the executive committee of Michael's Stores. When I first joined Michael's Corporate, the then CEO leading the organization, who had been there since 1996, had made it a requirement for each of us on the executive committee to have what I soon came to refer to as "a physical from hell." This was an annual visit to the Cooper Clinic in Dallas, renowned for pioneering preventative medicine and proactive wellness.

The CEO at the time had made this physical more or less mandatory after his own experience with the early detection of prostate cancer for which he was able to be treated and therefore allowed to continue living a healthy, productive life. He was committed to preventative screenings and required each of the senior management team to undergo this annual "physical from hell" which involved about six hours of poking, prodding, and other sorts of 21st Century legal medical torture. Though these examinations were not inexpensive, Michael's Corporate supported the testing for us and our spouses, reflecting the CEO's conviction of their worth and is something I will never forget!

My personal commitment to fitness made this a worthwhile endeavor and I saw it as a good opportunity to gauge my health. Among other elements of the physical was a "stress test" which involved a running on a treadmill and assessed your health based on your ability to go longer and harder in duration while they watched your heart's reaction to the stress of the exercise. My wife hated the whole experience, but because of my orientation for running, I actually liked it. In fact I would train for the running stress test, wanting to perform better than the previous year. I looked forward to the treadmill test because I wanted to break the record. While I never broke the running record, at times I had to "ride" because of an injury and I did break the bike record held at the time, I still always made it into the top 2% for running. I enjoyed seeing my conditioning and my ability to improve.

These exams typically covered everything from routine blood and urine analysis to cholesterol levels and things like hearing, eyesight, etc. By 2007 I had undergone six of these intensive screenings and noticed that each year in addition to the regular tests, they would generally perform some sort of specialized exam. One year they might test bone density and the next year body fat, but every year there was something unique.

For each of the six years I had undergone the battery of tests and then visited with my physician afterward as he took me through my results. They were great about offering advice to patients to improve their health. They might advise you to see an optometrist or adjust your diet for cholesterol, or whatever was needed to keep you on track. Well, in year seven I was put through my paces and had "performed well" on the treadmill and all was good—or so I thought. Way back hours ago, as the appointment had first begun, my doctor had asked me, "Do you want to have an EBT test?"

"Sure," I answered, "I think I did one last year though ... do you think I need it?"

"It only takes about five minutes," he replied, "and is really the best we have to continue to measure and evaluate any build-up of plaque in arterial walls." He looked at my chart before continuing, "It looks like it is covered by your insurance. I think we should do it."

"Yeah, go for it," I nodded.

It was not a test we were originally planning to do, but it just came up and we did it. Afterward I entered the office like always to speak with my doctor about the results of each test. I was confident. I knew I was in good health and looked forward to the annual confirmation that I was on the right track.

On this day, however, he began going over the results of each screening without the usual banter. In that direct, transparent style of communication I so appreciate he looked at me and said, "Herb (we had become rather close if you will, and that was my nickname which most people referred to me by), we found what we believe to be is a fatty tumor. We are not concerned, but we want you to have it looked at."

My heart skipped a beat. My adrenalin surged.

"A tumor?" I shook my head in disbelief, "What kind of tumor? ... Where?"

"We're not concerned," he repeated, "but we found what we believe to be a fatty tumor located on your thymus gland."

"My what?" I asked, feeling something I can't quite describe form in the pit of my stomach.

"The thymus," he began, "it's a small organ just behind your sternum. It is located in the space between your lungs," he pointed to the spot on my chest as he spoke. "This space also contains the heart and part of the esophagus. The thymus gland sits a little bit above and just in front of your heart."

"Wow," I shook my head nervously, "really?"

The doctor's gaze was calm and encouraging.

"Are you sure it's fatty?" I asked.

"I don't know," he shook his head, "that's why we want to do the test."

I left his office with all sorts of thoughts spinning inside my head. My doctor had been reassuring, but I was ill at ease.

## YOU'VE GOT CANCER

Six days later I was having a procedure done by a vascular surgeon to evaluate the fatty thymus tumor arthroscopically. It was supposed to take about 45 minutes, and my wife had come along to drive me home after. A few hours in they came out to the waiting room to speak with her, not wanting to alarm her since they did not yet know what they were dealing with, but this was not going to be a routine biopsy after all.

Five hours after it had all begun, I came out of the operating room. When I woke up from the anesthesia I learned they had removed a cancerous tumor roughly the size of a golf ball from inside my chest—a Small B-Cell Non-Hodgins Lymphoma. I still bear the scar where they had to deflate one of my lungs to pull the entire tumor out through the side of my body and then scrape around trying to get every last malignant cell.

Thymus cancers are rare, attacking less than one person per 1.5 million people.[1] Out of nowhere, having had no real symptoms to cause concern and being in overall good health with a fairly high-level fitness, I underwent a routine annual physical and they had found a tumor. My "fatty tumor" as I noted, turned out to be Small B-Cell Non-Hodgkins Lymphoma cancer— quite a mouthful. My doctor very specifically told me, "Don't Google this, it will scare you. What you read about this disease online will mislead you."

## MY "FATTY TUMOR" TURNED OUT TO BE A SMALL B-CELL NON-HODGKINS LYMPHOMA CANCER

He continued, "The tumor we found in you is the size of a golf ball and you seem to be having no other remarkable symptoms. Typically we find them when they are more the size of a football and we are searching for it because the patient has presented with other symptoms."

I listened carefully, gathering from his words that I was in as good of a place as could be given the size of the tumor and being, relatively speaking, asymptomatic. That said, recent studies have the 5-year survival rate at only about 24-28%.[2] "Survival rate" sounds much more positive doesn't it? That's the way researchers present it, but it doesn't take too much thinking to arrive at the conclusion that a 24-28% survival rate translates to a 72-76% mortality rate. I didn't particularly like those odds. Especially considering that these rates also include people who are in remission and do not take into account a patient's age or at what stage their cancer is in upon diagnosis. So the reality of statistics could be considered even more grim. *Yeah,* I thought, *better not to Google.*

Thankfully, my tumor had not metastasized and the surgeon was able to remove it all. But because of the kind of cancer it was, my doctor determined that a combination of something called "R-Chop" for the chemotherapy mix and then radiation were necessary to fight the disease.

## THE BATTLE BEGINS

On October 4, 2007 I had surgery, and shortly thereafter I started the first of what would be four rounds of chemo. For the next several months I would make a regular trip into downtown Dallas every three weeks and be hooked up to a seven-hour R-Chop IV drip of a drug designed to kill cancer cells, but indiscriminate in its ability to slay all the other healthy cells it finds. To make matters really memorable, within the R-Chop I received Doxorubicin, known as the *Infamous Red Devil,* which made me pee red for some time—as if the seven-hour ordeal wasn't enough!

The treatments really zapped me. Each round slaughtered my strength, but I was determined to fight and win.

My wife and I were in denial—not about the diagnosis, but about the prognosis. It was the good kind of denial, the one determined to beat the odds because you leave your mind and will no other alternative.

30

Fact: I had cancer. Truth: we would live our lives as perfectly normal as we possibly could.

I was a runner who ran every day. No matter how tired or sick I felt from the treatments, I still ran every single day. In the beginning I continued to run 5-7 miles averaging about 7.5 minutes per mile. By December I was only able to run 2-3 miles per day and my average was down to around 12 minutes per mile. My wife would ride her bike alongside just to make sure I was okay.

She never gave me one minute of pity. That isn't to say she wasn't concerned or didn't care, but she knew me well. She knew I needed her to say, "Get your ass out of bed and go do what you need to do," every morning. She knew I needed her to hold me accountable to my determination.

I did the chemo through the first of January, then took a break for a few days before starting 20 rounds of radiation. One treatment every day with weekends off. In the middle of the day I had to leave work, drive 20 miles downtown through traffic and lie completely still on a table to receive the radiation. They built a mask to the exact replica of my face. They would place this mask a mere eighth of an inch from my skin, then bolt it down to the table so I could not move my head even a millimeter. The location of the tumor was very near the heart, so they had to aim the radiation with great accuracy to ensure cancer cells in the area would be zapped without irradiating the muscles of my heart. Like chemo, radiation is equally tough on your body and it had mounting ramifications over time.

Each time I went in for a treatment it felt like I had to lie on that table for an eternity. It was uncomfortable—not just to my body, but in other ways as well. In reality each procedure wasn't very long, and I was probably on the table for only about 10 minutes give or take. But from the moment the mask was bolted down I felt like a prisoner, my subconscious calculating the risk/reward for radiation entering my body. One of my hobbies was car racing, (I know something tame and risk-free) and I had been racing at that point for about 10 years already. To pass the time, and to make the moment manageable, I ran one of my favorite tracks over and over in my head, every shift, every turn visualized as well as one could. I typically ran 5-7 laps and before long, the treatment had passed. *You want the cancer dead. You want the rest of your body alive. Deal with it,* I told myself.

The treatments made me incredibly tired. I had no appetite but was taking steroids, and although I gained only eight pounds I looked puffy, and not like myself. The stress of working all day, driving into the city for radiation then back to the office to work was a lot. I did not really know it, but later on my wife share with me how it took its toll.

## DETERMINED TO WIN

I lost all my hair and was bald. I was swollen and tired and my skin even appeared a little green, or so my better half told me long after this experience had passed. I really didn't look all that great, but still my wife gave me no pity. Her drive was kindness.

I went to work every day. At this time, Brian Cornell was the CEO of Michael's (now the CEO of Target). I am grateful he was at the helm during my ordeal. He allowed me to continue working, but around 3:00 pm every day he would walk by my office and check on me. On some days he would say, "You look like hell. Go home. Take care of yourself, not us."

I would drive myself home and crawl into bed, totally spent. For the rest of the day it was lights out. I was unwilling to give the cancer an inch, but yielded to wisdom in allowing my body rest to fight at the cellular level what the positivity of my mind could not reach.

Working was an outlet for me. I had the usual questions those with this disease face: *Is the cancer gone? Is it going to come back? What does this mean for me, for my family?* By focusing on work and running every day like I always had, I persevered. I stayed focused on the potential of my future and would not give in to the struggle I was facing in my present. I occupied my mind by living.

The first two years following diagnosis and treatment have the potential for the worst—death. These first two years also carry the greatest likelihood for the cancer to return. Because of this, I was screened every quarter to make sure the cancer had not come back.

**TENACITY AND ENDURANCE WERE KEY INGREDIENTS IN WHY I AM STILL ALIVE**

For those who survive, the next two to five years see better odds and you only need to be screened every six months. After five years your odds improve even more and unless you have a symptom that would cause concern, they only check you out once a year.

Leading up to each CT screening or PET scan I faced great trepidation, but the reality is I went about my life and lived it as normally as I could. The alternative was to freak out and that held absolutely no appeal to me.

I am now almost 11 years out from my diagnosis with no recurrence of cancer, but facing and fighting this disease changed me. It brought established priorities into even sharper focus and caused me to live with ever-increasing intention. The lessons I had learned and the character developed prior to my diagnosis brought me tenacity and endurance during my fight. They were a key ingredient, I believe, to why I am still alive. The lessons I learned and the clarity I gained while fighting and beating that disease have brought me wisdom and a perspective that continue to balance my decisions and guide my conduct.

# RESPOND WITH RESILIENCE

The only given is that whatever you expect to happen is not going to happen as you expect it. It might be better or it might be worse, but it will never be as expected. Your ability to learn through the unexpected will grow your leadership capacity. As a leader, you must choose between a thoughtful, measured approach to setbacks or creating a fire drill—responding with an inappropriate level of action which may appear as though you are working hard to change the outcome, when in reality you are just "making the fur fly." Scrambling around may feel like you are doing a lot when in reality you haven't done anything that improves the state of affairs at all.

To be able to assess the situation, regroup, and respond strategically, there is great advice provided in *Leadership on the Line.*[3] The concept is that a leader must leave the dance floor and go up to the balcony and look down. Only by removing yourself from the fray can you understand all the moving parts; see patterns and causes to gain clear perspective of the situation. Once an assessment is made, then you must return to the dance floor to guide the response and direct the motion. You must be able to remove yourself from the situation—almost like an out of body experience—to make thoughtful decisions. Then you must return to the situation to execute those decisions. This practice of "going up to the balcony" is wise in every situation, but never more so than in the midst of adversity.

Leaders are born and leaders are made. I think it takes a bit of both nature and nurture to balance these scales. In adversity leaders rise and take action rather than become immobilized by the challenges they face. Setbacks are a given—in business, in relationships, in life. When you develop resilience, the ability to bounce back after a setback, you increase your capacity to navigate the challenges leaders face. Your response to adversity is paramount to your ability to lead others well through stress, change, and uncertainty. Every challenge, whether it comes as a sharp decline in sales or battling cancer, is an opportunity to grow. Setbacks provide you the chance to persevere. Tenacity is an important ingredient to incubate innovation. Resilience through setbacks provides you with a sense of self-efficacy that impacts your confidence to execute goals even in the midst of trials.

As I consider the role of resilience in leadership, I realize that the themes of optimism, tenacity, endurance, and determination emerge no matter what topic I discuss. Any leader who stands the test of time possesses each of these in a healthy measure.

And now let's turn our attention to the bedrock core of all leadership—communication.

## ENDNOTES

1. *Thymoma and Thymic Carcinoma: Statistics.* © 2005-2018 American Society of Clinical Oncology (ASCO). Approved by the Cancer.net Editorial Board 1/2018. https://www.cancer.net/cancer-types/thymoma-and-thymic-carcinoma/statistics. Web. Retrieved 18 July, 2018.

2. *Thymoma and Thymic Carcinoma: Stages and Classification.* © 2005-2018 American Society of Clinical Oncology (ASCO). Approved by the Cancer.net Editorial Board 12/2017. https://www.cancer.net/cancer-types/thymoma-and-thymic-carcinoma/stages-and-classification. Web. Retrieved 18 July, 2018.

3. Heifitz, Ronald A., and Marty Linsky. *Leadership on the Line.* Harvard Business Review Press, 2002.

# YOUR RESPONSE TO SETBACKS IS PARAMOUNT TO YOUR ABILITY TO LEAD WELL

# Chapter Three

# COMMUNICATION
## THE ROSETTA STONE OF LEADERSHIP

"Everybody is watching you every minute anyway. If they think the message you're sending out is phony, they're going to say, 'Who does he think he is?' It's again, good business. But it is also an obligation."

**JAMES SINEGAL**
Co-Founder and former CEO of Costco

How you say something is every bit as important as what you are saying.

When my doctor sat across from me that day and delivered the diagnosis of cancer, how I received that news had a lot to do with his delivery of the information. Picture a tall man, at least 6'6" with a commanding presence, a head full of wisdom-whitened hair, and dressed as a physician should so that even his clothing communicated authority. His posture was open as he sat in front of me, shoulders back, head up, and he looked me in the eye man-to-man as he gave me this rotten news.

There was empathy in him as he said, "Listen, Herb, you've got cancer and it is a tough, rare cancer. You're a bit older than most people when we found this thing, and it has a pretty high mortality rate."

There was no doubt in my mind that he was telling the truth straight up, no sugar coating. So, I trusted him when he continued, "I don't want you to Google this thing because what you are going to find about this disease will scare the hell out of you …" and he went on to tell me some of the ugly statistics.

"But," he offered hope, "you are not one them. We found your tumor early and we have a treatment plan to cure this thing. You are going to make it."

With far more meaning than his words alone could have provided, he had communicated the bigger picture to me with his tone of voice, his facial expressions, body language, and even his posture. All these things working together is what produced the flow and exchange of the information I needed to create a greater understanding. I left that conversation fully aware of what was in front of me, what the most desirable outcome would be, and how we were going to work together to achieve that.

This is the essence of communication.

## TONE OF VOICE

Tone of voice is a key indicator of meaning. As much as I try to choose my words carefully, I also try to speak calmly and in even tones that reassure those listening that I am comfortable, confident, and composed. As a practice, I don't raise my voice. I don't typically use swear words or vulgarities. That said, every once in a purple moon I do elevate my volume in an emotional moment or use an expletive, and when I do people clearly recognize something is different and pay attention. It's a signaling moment, and intended or not, it clearly conveys a different kind of communication.

In these instances, my divergence in tone serves to punctuate something powerful. A raised voice as punctuation can be a strong communication tool. A raised voice as normal practice is an angry guy no one cares to listen to. People take important cues from the timbre of your voice. Tone matters.

# BODY LANGUAGE

Had my doctor kept his eyes on my chart instead of holding my gaze, I might have felt he had something to hide, like there was more to the story than he was willing to share. But he sat up straight and tall when he spoke to me, so even in my subconscious I was aware he was speaking from experience and with authority.

Body language communicates a great many things we interpret in the moment without even giving them much thought. Arms crossed over the body, they are defensive. Fidgeting or eyes darting around, they are bored looking for an exit. Someone who gives you no personal space is either angry or seeking to dominate the conversation.

You don't need to be a body language expert to read and interpret the cues. That said, just a little heightening of your awareness can help you better connect with others and make sure your meaning isn't getting lost because of your demeanor.

When I am in a meeting, I have noticed that when I am sitting upright and at the back of my chair and the meeting is just moving along with conversation—the typical dialogue and interaction—all seems to be more or less status quo. But, if I move and go from sitting upright at the back of my chair to adjust my position forward so I am now half-off my chair, elbows on my knees, chin resting in the upstretched palm of my hands, suddenly the conversation takes on a different *je ne sais quoi*. Whomever I am talking to and whatever we are talking about experiences the shift, and the conversation instantly becomes more engaging and less intimidating. It's remarkable how much posture can impact the substance of the conversation. Your body talks.

## OPEN TO INTERPRETATION

Without effective communication, misunderstanding occurs. Whether the misconception is caused by misreading a minor nuance or from a total deviation of what was originally intended, the result produces a cascading domino effect of confusion. If as much energy were devoted to providing clear, transparent communication to begin with as is required to alleviate or minimize the effects of vague communication, we would all be much better off.

Comprehension is arrived at through a process of interpretation. The various elements of communication: words, body language, and tone as well as the nuances of context, history, and actions all provide a cumulative filter through which the meaning of words is derived. The challenge is to accomplish understanding with which to take action in a mutually agreeable way. Clear, straightforward communication best achieves this goal. On the flip side, when people are unwilling to communicate directly, then parties hear what they want to hear or what they think they hear resulting in mistakes, offenses, decreased productivity, low morale, and a host of other undesirable outcomes. I contend that poor communication can be worse than no communication at all. As a leader, it is important to communicate clearly, consistently, and often.

## COMMUNICATE CLEARLY

The more precise, crisp, and succinct your communication, the more likely people will understand it. Often things are crystal clear in my own mind, but because I can get wordy in my expression, this clarity does not always translate to those listening. I have an awareness of this tendency, so when communicating instructions or directives I work to be more concise, weighing my words to be sure my meaning is clear to others. And when I am done I often say, "Tell me what you heard. Tell me what I said, or at least how you interpreted what I said." This gives me (and them) a chance to check in and validate a two-way process of reaching a mutual understanding.

A leader's communication is often a balancing act of what vs. why. The why is where passion and energy around a vision naturally lend itself to great storytelling. While this can be incredibly inspirational in conveying why, it does not necessarily clearly define what: What comes next? What action needs to be taken? What problem needs to be solved? To communicate the what, specific statements with well-defined implication better convey clear meaning.

For example, say there is an earthquake. The moment requires, "Get under your desk now!" Clarity here is best achieved through brevity. But say you have been troubled by the homeless situation in your community and want to enlist the help of others to make a difference. In that scenario, crafting a story about how you see it, why it is important to you, and what you think can be done by working together is better for meeting the broader challenge of getting people on board behind your cause. Unlike the earthquake example, this condition calls for narrative and storytelling to achieve the purpose. This example around the homeless clearly requires dialogue, engaging in meaningful two-way interaction, and communication does not begin and end in one brief moment. Both require clear communication, but the context of how this is best achieved is drastically different.

# COMMUNICATE CONSISTENTLY

How you communicate— the level of trust, knowledge, the ability to create understanding—is built off the belief that *what you say* and the *way you say it* is consistent moment to moment, event to event. Otherwise, people have to figure out what your communication orientation is today vs. what it was a month ago. If you are always straightforward, transparent, and direct, your words can be taken at face value. It is established that you mean what you say and you say what you mean, and that you will share information appropriately to achieve successful outcomes. Your communication is therefore trustworthy and reliable. Show me a leader who tells their team everything needed to know one minute and does not communicate at all the next and I'll show you a team that is in crisis. Inconsistent communication equates to inconsistent performance. Trust breaks down, respect crumbles, and results fade.

# COMMUNICATE OFTEN

Business in the modern age happens at an incredible pace. To believe you can communicate infrequently and create mutual understanding is a myth. Communicating often is as important as communicating clearly and consistently. This is how leaders keep everyone walking down the same path toward the same goal.

You have heard that knowledge is power, and so it is. Dictators control access to knowledge to maintain their power. "If I have the knowledge and you don't, I have power over you." But servant-level leaders know that communicating often creates understanding. By sharing your knowledge (your power) you are empowering people. This generosity of knowledge and information through daily, weekly, and important "moment-in-time" communications

**COMMUNICATING OFTEN IS AS IMPORTANT AS COMMUNICATING CLEARLY AND CONSISTENTLY**

are all unequivocally important touch points through which you can successfully communicate.

## TELL THEM AGAIN, AND THEN AGAIN WRITE DOWN WHAT YOU SAID

There is only so much information people can factually absorb at one moment. In an hour of discussion, two or three meaty things is probably the limit of capacity for hearing, grasping, and remembering. If one tries to communicate ten things that are all rather robust and deep, chances are people probably cannot absorb them all. One way to communicate and ensure that information is heard and absorbed is by repeating it over and over. There is a core Athenian concept which was picked up by the Romans who turned it into a proverb: "*repetitio est mater studiorum*," or "repetition is the mother of all learning." In my mind, this is critically important. Say too much and each person will remember different things. Say the same thing over and over, and people will understand it's important. Additionally, if you need to cover more ground topically, it is best when this is supported with documentation.

When I served as the CEO of Blue Nile, I provided weekly communication in sound bytes that was topical, of the moment, and focused on no more than one or two important things. But every six weeks or so, I held town hall meetings which were visionary at a high-level and shared inspiring elements of what the company was working on. I could cover more things that were broader in scope in this forum. By repeating the really critical elements and then following this up with documentation, the written context of our vision, mission, strategy, and the operating plan was clearly communicated throughout the management ranks. This gave everyone the ability to cascade that communication down without losing or changing the meaning.

Written communication allows people to look at it, reflect, and ask questions for clarity and understanding. It removes ambiguity and allows every member of the team to engage meaningfully with the messaging. From billboards to business cards, memos to wall art, the power of the written word allows the message to be repeated clearly so hopefully, the meaning can resonate more strongly.

## TELL THEM CAREFULLY, WRITE DOWN WHAT YOU MEAN TO SAY

There is a certain authenticity to engaging with someone in unscripted dialogue. However, the higher up you go the more people trade on your words. So the minute you let your guard down and don't think enough about the words you choose, the way you present yourself, or the tone you use, you may find your unscripted communication can also result in unintended consequences.

During my tenure at Blue Nile, we were a public company, so transcriptions of our earnings calls were documented for the world to see. Every word said on a call was recorded. Investors and analysts would have meetings with me after the calls and would often ask me about two or three specific sentences out of the entire transcript. For the most part, we scripted comments we wanted to share in advance. Knowing these would be documented and available for review made us very thoughtful and articulate to ensure we were saying what we intended to say.

At some point, we would open the call up for questions from people who were listening live, so our answers had to be unscripted. Of course, we did our best to answer these openly, transparently, eloquently, and crisply. But no matter how well you do, the likelihood you may say something you didn't intend to is high. Inevitably these words will be taken out of context and could be received in an entirely different way than intended.

I have learned that what is said in a public setting is incredibly important. People read much into it, and in the case of my role at Blue Nile, even casual comments could affect stock trades and interfere with investor confidence. In a setting that is not public, such as with employees or partners, you are more likely to be given the benefit of the doubt in a moment of misspeaking, but what you wear, your posture and body language, how articulate you are in the way you communicate all add up. Say what you mean to say.

## THE COMMUNICATION OF COMMITMENT

Thankfully, my leadership style has never come across as some sort of "snake oil salesman" working an angle. I highly value that people believe I am genuine and sincere when I communicate, not selling them a bill of goods. This stems from my consistent actions. Certain kinds of actions are the greatest example of commitment.

I had cancer, you have read that part of my story. So I understand how painful it is for people to receive a cancer diagnosis and how hard it is on them, their family, and the community to which they belong. I was lucky with the outcome of my treatment and grateful that I am still here many years after having been diagnosed. In my own way, my gratitude for overcoming this disease led me to want to impact other people having cancer. I believe I can make a difference.

To that end, I joined a charity ride in Seattle to raise money for cancer research. My passion for riding and my desire to make a difference for those battling cancer merged into this tangible expression. I went from riding 50 miles for the cause to riding 165 miles because I could raise

more money by this longer commitment. I became an advisor for the charity and went on to solicit everybody and their mother, brother, sister, or uncle to help with the cause. I sent out dozens of emails about my fundraising eventually, appealing with, "I am sorry if I am bothering you, but this is important. In fact, it's really about life or death." I was actually totally okay with being a pest, the reality is that one out of every two men and one out of three women will be diagnosed with some sort of cancer in their lifetime, so raising money really was (and is) a matter of life and death for many. My plea was authentic in expressing this very particular passion born from my personal experience.

This fervency has made my communication direct, maybe even blunt about desiring to raise money for cancer research. My actions further backed up my communication. I was directly involved in the cause to raise money and I demonstrated this by my commitment to ride 165 miles and climb 10,000 feet in two days—not an easy undertaking. Rather than just saying, "Cancer is important to me to find a cure," and then writing out a check for $100 to a charity, my actions back up my commitment and demonstrate to others how important this is to me by all the things I am doing. Commitment is communicated by actions.

# COMMUNICATION CULTURE CONNECTION

To be successful at any level—as a parent, a business person, serving on a board, or functioning in any role as a leader means you are helping to set and create a vision for where you want to go and facilitate the ability for people to go there with you.

To be an effective leader you have to be an effective communicator, these go hand in hand. You really cannot be one without becoming the other. Whether written or spoken, your words and the way in which you communicate them create what your expectations are and the way people will interact with them. Communication creates the culture in which you live and work and that does not just happen, it is something that must be thoughtfully crafted and nurtured over time. Every element of core skills, wills, and values becomes embedded in the culture and these all come out of what you consistently communicate.

This is why I believe communication is the single most important element in leadership. Master the art of communication and you are well on the way to building something of value that will last. Communication is leadership's core.

As the leader, the team takes their cues from you. Your level of panic or steady calm informs their approach. A leader communicates all day, every day. Each of the remaining elements we will discuss "leak out" of your communication—both verbal and non-verbal, official and unofficial. Your attitude and approach are contagious and quickly spread through the ranks. With this in mind, I want to share an interesting twist on optimism and how a role model's impossible decision made a lasting impression on me.

**COMMUNICATION IS THE SINGLE MOST IMPORTANT ELEMENT IN LEADERSHIP**

Chapter Four

# OPTIMISM
## WHAT'S THE ALTERNATIVE? SERIOUSLY, WHY ASSUME SOMETHING BAD?

"Optimism is a strategy for making a better future because unless you believe that the future can be better, you are unlikely to step up and take responsibility for making it so."

**NOAM CHOMSKY**
The Father of Modern Linguistics, Cognitive Scientist

Optimism is not just a point of view—glass half empty or glass half full approach—optimism is a way of life. It impacts your every thought, word, and deed and therefore, has bearing on every person with whom you interact. Few people are likely to link the words "optimism" with "depression" in a discussion of one individual. This would likely seem an either/or proposition, and while this may indeed present a contradiction in terms, such was the case with my mother.

Family was everything to my mom. When she was young she had been a paralegal and graduated from college, but decided not to work or pursue a career in order to raise her family. We exemplified American small town values and she made sure we had clean clothing, daily hot cooked meals, and on Friday nights took us to Shabbat services. She created a loving, warm environment in which we were free to learn and grow. Family came first.

She and my father met and were married very young, and following the birth of one of her children, she began battling with depression, sometimes severe. Unless you have been around people who struggle with depression, it will be hard for you to relate to the impact severe depression has on every person who loves them. It is an inescapable daily reality. In spite of these challenges, she and my father were inseparable—loving each other and serving our family side-by-side for more than fifty years of marriage.

There were times when we went for weeks without any signs of her depression and everything felt normal. At other times it seemed to take all the energy she could muster just to get out of bed and make it through her daily routine. But because of her deep commitment to my father and to our family, she fought hard against her condition.

She saw a psychiatrist who provided counseling and addressed the issues which were emotional in nature, but she also sought the help of a psychopharmacologist. This was a doctor who specializes in the study of the effects of chemicals on the body and brain, and in addition to using counseling techniques, they also prescribe medication to treat patients suffering from mental disorders. In my mother's case, both emotional issues and a chemical imbalance were components of the depression against which she struggled for most of her adult life.

So, speaking of her in the context of a chapter on optimism may seem like a paradox to you. To me, she is the most natural example I can offer to illustrate the power of optimism and how it feeds determination, perseverance, and true grit.

# WHEN YOU THINK IT CAN'T GET ANY WORSE—IT USUALLY DOES

When my mom was 60, she was diagnosed with a very rare sarcoma. It was so terrible, in fact, that her options were pretty grave. Located in the ball of her foot, the sarcoma could be addressed in one of three ways: 1) she could have chemotherapy in the hopes of possibly killing the tumor; 2) they could try removing the tumor surgically, but she would likely never be able to walk on that foot again, or if she walked it would not be without pain and handicap; or, 3) they could amputate her leg below the knee. By removing the tumor and the area surrounding it, the cancer could not metastasize and spread elsewhere in her body. She would, essentially, be cancer free but down one leg.

It took her but moments to come to a decision, "Off with my leg!" she declared bravely.

Sure, she took it on the chin for about five minutes as the range of emotions played out in her mind but to her, surgery and amputation gave her the best chance for staying alive. A leg was a small thing to give up in exchange for the possibility of a long life ahead with her family.

Given her life-long battle with depression, this is a remarkable indication of her spirit. When faced with the radical decision to become an amputee at 60 with all the challenges of recovery and rehabilitation ahead, her optimism governed her will.

This optimism was never more evident than shortly after the amputation. The family went together on an Alaskan cruise to celebrate their fortieth wedding anniversary. We started calling her "Peg" in honor of her new peg-leg. She dressed up for her anniversary dinner and went right on celebrating by dancing that evening (or at least moving around to the music) with my father.

That isn't to say she lived happily ever after and never battled with depression again. She certainly did. As her only son, I had a special relationship with my mother and one night I found myself alone with her in the living room. She was really wrestling with depression at that time and striving to cope with the loss of her leg. It was an overwhelming situation. Having a history of depression coupled with the trauma of an amputation, she could easily have slipped into a very dark place and never come out. I will never forget how she sat up and said, "Screw this," and shifted her whole approach. She snapped back in, allowing her larger goals to overcome the pull to pity herself. She did not wallow, she won.

## THE POWER OF CHOICE

I have little doubt about where my own spirit of optimism originated.

 My zest for life, my own tenacity and perseverance is a testament to my mom and the DNA within me. She gave me my compass and taught me how to use it. From her I learned to make lemonade from lemons, and how once you have put your mind to something, you do it—you don't look back. Regrets are pointless.

It's true that none of us can control what life brings us, but we can make the choice for how we will approach each of those moments. Every day brings the opportunity to choose to be optimistic and have the spirit and energy to live in and for the moment, or make the choice to be downtrodden, a victim of circumstances, expecting the worst.

My mother's decisiveness in that hour has given me inspiration from which to draw ever since. In her mind, the answer was to live. Having a tumor equaled being crippled. Opting for chemotherapy equaled sickness and a high likelihood the cancer would spread. Choosing to have her leg off meant it was done. She could get on with the business of living.

When I faced my own battle with cancer, my decisiveness to fight and live was informed by my mother's spirit to live—just another setback through which to persevere. There is always a choice how to respond.

The choice is yours. Your approach to each moment governs your interactions with others, sets the tone, and impacts the level of creativity and resourcefulness with which you lead. Optimism opens you up to possibilities and therefore, accepts risk for the potential they bring. Like a magnet, optimism draws people to you in a spirit of cooperation and lends itself to a positive work culture.

Those who have the "glass is half empty" mentality also seem to expect leaks in the glass, or for the glass to break and empty out completely. They play with worst-case scenarios and their grim predictions often prove self-fulfilling. This only serves to reinforce their negative approach. In work environments, they have trouble trusting others or sharing information. They tend to deflect blame and prognosticate problems. This does not lend itself to innovation or ingenuity.

For me the choice is clear. I surround myself with positive people.

## OPPORTUNITY IN EVERY DIFFICULTY

"A pessimist is someone who finds difficulty in every opportunity, an optimist finds opportunity in every difficulty."

**ABRAHAM LINCOLN**

Dr. Jack Singer, who performs cutting-edge research in the field of Performance Enhancement, wrote an intriguing article called *The Terrific Power of Optimism in Sports Success* in which he highlights differences in athletic performance based on an athlete's orientation either toward pessimism or optimism.

He makes his case sharing research done by Dr. Martin Seligman showing how pessimistic athletes and teams believe that losses and poor performance during crunch times reflect their lack of ability to succeed. These athletes equate outside forces—things such as poor weather conditions, a string of missed shots, unfair calls by a referee, or even a belief that their opponent is cheating, as the reason they fail. This negative interpretation of difficulties causes them to become angry, tighten up, and thus fulfill their own prophecies as their performance continues to weaken. Their last loss causes them to expect to lose the next time, and the cycle repeats.

However, athletes facing the same kind of temporary setbacks but with an optimistic outlook tend to re-focus and actually improve their performance. Rather than blaming negative or distracting circumstances for a setback, they instead see their internal dialogue as key in responding to them. They feel empowered, not helpless. They will adjust their thinking and change their game plan in order to recapture momentum and win. Even if they do suffer a loss, they tend to learn from it. They will change their internal thoughts, and expect to win the next time … which they usually go on to do.[1]

The Super Bowl comeback of the New England Patriots against the Atlanta Falcons in 2017 illustrates this point effectively. This game will undoubtedly go down in history as one of the most remarkable comebacks of all time. Down 28-3 in the third quarter, most thought a win for Atlanta was inevitable. No team had ever won a Super Bowl after trailing more than 10 points. There was no way a win for New England was a realistic possibility, but I guess no one told Tom Brady and the team. They refused to believe victory was not within their reach and continued playing at a level that demonstrated their conviction that a great outcome was possible.

They went on to score 31 unanswered points against the Falcons. The world watched in disbelief, and no matter how you feel about the Patriots, you have to tip your hat to this incredible display of drive. The power of positive thinking—pure optimism—is unquestionably key in New England's winning performance. As Disney animator Marc Davis says, "All it takes is all you've got."

## BELIEF IN BUSINESS

As much as optimism plays a part in sports performance, it also affects business performance. Let's shift our focus from the field of play to the world of work. As a leader, a critical core skill is to inspire and motivate others, rallying them behind vision and mission. If you don't believe, why should anyone else?

Each and every day, your team looks to you for signals. Your level of energy and optimism drives the atmosphere for the whole team. Everyone is taking their cues from you, so when you believe in the possible, this optimism propels the whole team.

An e-commerce company on the leading edge of retail, things were not that great when I first came on board the team at Blue Nile. From 2007 to 2011 the company had grown less than 10% in total revenue, and by the fourth quarter of 2011 (just before I joined), sales revenue was at -2.1% … not a great performance.

Add to this total picture of sales that had not grown measurably for the prior four years, employee turnover was significantly up. The company was under increasing pressure and there were significant challenges within the organization. Some of these elements were somewhat daunting. That said, during the year-end, fourth-quarter earnings call for 2011, Blue Nile's founder, Mark Vadon, had addressed these challenges candidly and also commented on opportunities.

As a retailer and public company, Blue Nile's role was (and continues to be) to create a different kind of relationship with the consumer. To be both innovative and disruptive is the essence of the company's founding. Mark's vision was to exceed our customer's expectations and to create healthy returns for our shareholders.

On that 2011 fourth quarter call, even in the middle of all the challenges, Mark managed to create a feeling of optimism for the business and generate enthusiasm. He did this in a number of ways, but something that stood out to me at a high level was that Mark thanked the team for the hard work they had put in during Q4, not only to run the business but of equal importance, to reignite sales. His comments acknowledged publicly, and dare I say, in a direct, transparent, and possibly vulnerable way, areas he believed where he and the team had potentially mis-stepped in trying to optimize the business too soon in its life cycle.

He went on to talk about clear areas where investment was needed to grow the business into a much larger entity and how to make those investments grow, then optimize once the company was much larger. He acknowledged his belief that this was going to be the most effective way to deeply engage the consumers with Blue Nile—both the brand and as a retailer—to create long-term value for the shareholders. He closed the call by underlining his belief in the process they had gone through to put together this planning cycle to build the business to become much larger.

Mark was open and honest about the challenges, but presented genuine enthusiasm for the opportunities that lay ahead. He communicated his optimism for their potential without hyperbole or using an overzealous tone. He was authentic and humble.

At that time, Mark had stepped in and as the Chairman he assisted the then interim CEO, so as I took the baton for this sales-challenged, margin-depressed, high-employee-turnover entity, I knew I was taking on a company ripe with challenges, but equally so with opportunities. Mark had communicated a spirit of optimism clearly and genuinely, and in the midst of uncertainty and fear, hope was beginning to stir when I came aboard on March 30, 2012.

Let's be honest, the optimism present in Mark on the call was not necessarily apparent down through the ranks at that moment. During the previous few years, the drumbeat had gotten lost in translation. Results took a beating as the team was taking their direction and executing vision through a one-way channel of communication. At the time I was asked to come on board, the work culture of Blue Nile had become fear-based. Concern over retribution and reprisals had squelched creativity and resourcefulness. Teams were disjointed and unity was fractured.

I shared earlier how I interviewed 100 people on the corporate staff and took time looking, listening, and learning. Eventually I held that town hall meeting where I shared the plan Mark laid out in light of what I had also learned from them, how we would go about executing the plan, and the changes which needed to be made. I genuinely believed we could change the culture and see results. I had encountered them individually and borne witness to their talents and strengths. I knew that if we pooled these together behind clearly defined, well-understood goals, things would turn around.

My direct, transparent tone played well. I was sincere in my optimism and my communication was genuine. I believed what I was saying. I had just joined the company knowing the challenges, but was ecstatic about the opportunities. To seize them, I needed for all of us to row together and in sync. First believe, then achieve.

During the remaining three quarters in 2012 we delivered results which raised the year-end performance to more than a 15% increase from that 2011 Q4 call. Our turnover dropped 40% and while everything was not perfect, we were on the right track. We believed. We had a positive spirit and optimism that had not been around for some time. The Blue Nile team was on it! It was exciting and we could see that there was a path forward. The second year added to this spirit and optimism, and we delivered just under a 15% increase again over where we had ended in 2012. Employee turnover dropped another 36%, and was now hovering around 16% annually. Quite a turnaround! We now had an engaged staff, a committed team, and our culture was evolving positively. Optimism for the future was great.

## BELIEVE IT UNTIL IT BECOMES SO

Leaders are privy to the big picture. Leaders have the responsibility to leave the dance floor, go to the balcony, and return with an informed view of the situation.[3] Seeing it all requires a certain pragmatism. Optimism does not mean "pipe dreamer." Optimism represents a genuine belief that "where there's a will, there's a way." Henry Ford said, "If you think you can do a thing or think you can't, you're right." If you believe you will win, then nine times out of ten, you will win.

I joined Blue Nile because of my belief in the business opportunity in spite of the challenges. To that end, I was confident in my communication. Confidence is not arrogance or bravado, it is firm trust—a belief in the favorable outcome that is solid enough to make you commit to the process, however arduous, to see the result achieved.

Even when the business was not yet working, I believed. That belief was genuine enough on a personal level to translate large enough for other people to see and buy in and believe it with me. My belief was a forceful extroversion of myself, if you will. I had to demonstrate a hyper-belief in order for people to want to get behind that—I acted as though it already was what I believed it could become.

Hyperbole won't play. The belief has got to be genuine. The optimism real, unwavering when reports are good or bad. But when you are sincere and your commitment to the outcome is steadfast, even when reports are not good or there is a wobble in performance, those following you will allow some leniency, trusting with you that an applied course over time will yield the desired results.

As a leader, the challenge in turning things around is to create small wins to build big wins to create momentum. You don't try to come back from an unbroken losing streak by swinging for the fences. Instead of going for a home run you first go for the single. Just get on base. This then opens the opportunity to win. The small victory creates hope and a rallying point around the vision to get the team moving in the right direction. Optimism is the faith that leads to achievement.[2]

When you live with hope and possibilities flowing through your veins, every decision you make and action you take inspires those whom you lead. Optimism is so much more than a core value, it is a state of being. All my core values are informed by optimism. The values a leader holds—their definition of True North—impacts those they lead in a more direct way than their gender, age, education, or even experience. In the next chapter, I will introduce you to Scott Hessler, former Vice Chairman of Carter Hawley Hale, and share ways in which he stretched me to grow and how his influence has impacted my entire career. We will talk meaningfully about our values and discuss how to grow them in a more positive direction through each new experience.

## ENDNOTES

1. *The Terrific Power of Optimism in Sports Success.* © 2017. Jack Singer, Ph.D. Web. http://drjacksinger.com/the-terrific-power-of-optimism-in-sports-success/. Retrieved 23 July 2018.
2. This quote is attributed to Helen Keller.
3. Heifitz, Ronald A., and Marty Linsky. *Leadership on the Line.* Harvard Business Review Press, 2002.

OPTIMISM IMPACTS YOUR EVERY THOUGHT,
WORD, AND DEED, AND THEREFORE,
HAS BEARING ON EVERY PERSON
WITH WHOM YOU INTERACT

Chapter Five

# VALUES
## TRUE NORTH ... OR SLIGHTLY NORTHEAST AND IN A GENERALLY NORTHERN DIRECTION

"I never wanted to be on any billionaires list.
I never define myself by net worth. I always
try to define myself by my values."

**HOWARD SCHULTZ**
Former CEO and Executive Chairman of Starbucks

It may sound cliché, but when I die, I don't want to be just a name on a tombstone sitting in some cemetery somewhere. At this point I am confident I won't have the global impact of someone like Oprah Winfrey or Jeff Bezos, but I hope to make a lasting impression and have a positive impact on the people with whom I am privileged to interact. During my life, I want to have created some enduring mark on the world, even if only for a small microcosm of people. Many people have influenced me along the way, and a handful of those have left a distinct imprint on my life and helped to shape who I have become. Their mentoring helped further impact and further fine tune my belief in values which have become the core essence of who I am.

This idea—making a lasting impact—is central to my values system, and therefore a discussion of this for me is less about examining individual values such as respect, honor, tenacity, positivity, etc., and more about sharing my thoughts regarding the foundation of those values—the bedrock for how all these core tenets have framed my life and, in reality, shape all our lives. Our values guide how we work and relate to others. I believe my True North is to do good and make an impact. This conviction points me toward embracing values that are congruent with this mission. Because I desire to have a positive impact on my family, on people I work with, and on those with whom I share life as part of a community, I adhere to values that are consistent with doing good and making an impact. I want to do more than take up air and occupy space, and while I do enjoy life—I make a good living and love having fun—that isn't enough for me. I seek to invest in the world. I desire to give back in meaningful ways which represent a purpose more significant than my own existence and far less fleeting than my personal enjoyment.

## STRETCHED TO GROW

When I was young, my very first job was as an executive trainee at Carter Hawley Hale Department Stores, based in Los Angeles. I had the privilege of working for Scott Hessler, a senior executive who, in time, became the Vice Chairman. Having begun his career in home merchandising, he had grown into an influential figure in retail—a merchant's merchant, respected and trusted. This man had a significant impact on my life which still has a considerable bearing on me some thirty years later. He demonstrated to me what mentorship looked like. His intentionality in the development of people and their potential became a model for me as to what it was to be a true champion of growth. I loved how he effectively supported people while always seeming to do the right thing.

Now understand, while I was working as a department manager for a retail store location, Scott Hessler was serving as an executive vice president of the company. He was a genius at what he did, and the gap between us was enormous. There had to have been about ten layers or more between his position and mine, but his passion for people and product made him notice what was happening in the company down through all the levels.

I was this twenty-three-year-old guy running a department selling china, crystal, flatware, lamps, picture frames … not a category I had a lot of experience with even as a customer, nevertheless, I led a team of sales associates and the department's assistant manager and together we changed the business results. Our department went from being ranked thirteenth out of forty-two to becoming one of the top performing stores. Mr. Hessler became interested in understanding what we were doing to change the business and in that process got to know me well. He took a liking to me and noticed the results I was creating through my leadership in a tangible, intuitive way, and so he began to mentor me. Scott modeled for me how to listen, engage, and produce results. He taught me how to ask questions and be inquisitive, encouraged me to be open to failure, and exposed me to a wide range of experiences. During my time at Carter Hawley Hale, Scott was moved into the role of Vice Chairman, but he still continued to mentor and guide me. Throughout this mentorship, he moved me across eight different jobs in nine years. At points in time, I know people thought he was crazy.

In the first move, Mr. Hessler placed me into corporate as an assistant buyer in the linen staples department. Here I encountered a difficult personality in my direct reporting relationship with the buyer. There was no support behind my ideas or actions no matter how much time I spent on specific analytic review. Because I was relatively new to the business, I had a fresh perspective which afforded me the ability to look at things differently from other vantage points. A typical response from this leader was to have my reports scribbled all over or even ripped up and returned with comments such as, "Where did you come up with this? I don't think this will work ... I don't agree ... but you go ahead and do it." If margins and revenue were stellar as a result of one of these promotions, this person would take the credit. But if something at any level proved to be a misstep, I could count on retribution. It's crazy to me looking back, how successful this buyer's "numbers" were and yet how bad her skills were as a manager, leader, and boss. My quality of interaction became so low that I could do nothing right in her eyes. Still, I took the high road. I chose to soldier on and to let things go. Though I could just as easily have gone to HR, I chose not to and instead, at least for the time being, rode this out, learning as much what not to do as I could have learned what to do.

Over time I had become so miserable that I actually placed a call to Target's corporate office and had been lucky enough to have a phone interview. Post that call they suggested if I was going to be in town to let them know. Thanksgiving was approaching and we decided to take the family home to Minnesota. By then I had grown quite weary of the situation, so just before our trip I called Target again to see if there might now be an opening available for an assistant buyer. As luck would have it, I met with them and received a job offer. I returned to Los Angeles shortly thereafter and handed in my resignation.

"You can't go," Scott said when he learned of my decision, "why have you chosen to do this?"

"Listen," I replied, "after eight months I have felt no progress with this person, we have no alignment of ideas, and things here are just not resonating with me. I have tried to change the way things are, but there was no movement. It's untenable, and so it makes sense for me to move on."

Though I had begun in a retail store managing the hard home departments and was grateful to have been promoted to this position as an assistant buyer in linen staples, it had grown unbearable. In response, Scott moved me out of that situation (later that executive was fired), and made me an assistant buyer in the junior's clothing department. This provided a tremendous opportunity to regroup and a chance to experience fashion merchandising while I encountered a completely different pace for business—a bonus. While there I worked for Halle Redman, a leader who genuinely lived out Scott's school of mentorship and leader development creating even greater learning experiences that proved an accelerant for my career. Based on the quality of my work in that assistant buyer's role and the success experienced in my merchandising responsibility there, I was elevated to the full buyer's role.

In my position as a buyer in the junior's department, I continued to experience good results. Based on these achievements, I was moved back to home to fix fashion bedding. From there I was placed over the department for newborns and infants, then spent some time working in young girl's apparel before being sent across to young men's clothing and then finally in my last role, I was asked to help lead and develop the planning and allocation function. In this newly created role of "Vice President for Planning and Allocation for Women's Apparel and Special Sizes," I was literally helping create and drive a completely new core function. Talk about moving me around and stretching me!

**MY MENTOR SAW THINGS IN ME AND STRETCHED ME IN WAYS THAT CHALLENGED ME TO GROW**

When questioned why he moved me around so much Scott would say, "He is going to be one of our senior leaders," and kept pushing me to a place that made me (and others) uncomfortable. Yet even while being challenged, I relished the courtesy he extended to me and his orientation to stretch me in ways that others thought were unrealistic. He saw something in me and was kind enough to call it out.

At the timing of each of these transitions, I knew very little about the product categories where Scott was placing me, but they were each to some degree a broken business. I understood business, and I had a knack for fixing them.

During my tenure at Carter Hawley Hale, I worked for really great people, and to this day that understanding and belief in the impact someone can make on you has never left me. Long after I did eventually move on, I continued to connect with Scott once or twice a year until he passed away. His influence on me impacted my entire career. He was the kind of leader I love to follow, the kind I aspire to be. He pushed me to become a better version of myself and constantly increased my capacity and improved my skills. I talk about him and his impact often, and I still draw from how he mentored me.

Scott Hessler made a lasting impression on me and others. Thirty years down the road his approach to leadership still serves as a guide for me. He is a valuable reference point on my compass—he did good and made a lasting, positive impact. That is precisely what I want to do.

## LEAD AT ANY LEVEL

I believe we can lead at any level; with or without a title, even with the absence of formal structure or recognition. The alternative is to become just another voice doing something that will change nothing. You can be a leader to the degree that the world in which you live can be impacted by your values and orientation. These values consistently lived out cause people to follow you. If you are the one holding the compass and certain of your bearings, then you are who they will look to for guidance. If you have a genuine desire to help others along the path, then no matter who you are, what role you play, or how far up or down the totem pole you maybe—you are the one they will follow. A confident, caring voice brings clarity and comfort. Values demonstrate who you are. The soft ability to influence others comes naturally from consistently living your values before them.

Leadership isn't just people responding to you in a chain of command. People looking up to you for some reason to guide them in any area equates to leadership. How you speak to others, your work ethic, and how you interact with people all demonstrate something. Hopefully, this creates a wake for people to get in and follow you. They don't have to report to you formally, but instead, they recognize things they like about you and desire to emulate. This is a more authentic leadership than the kind one can have simply by bearing the title of CEO. You can be a CEO and still be a terrible leader. You can be a terrific leader without bearing any recognized "leadership" title, even a title such as CEO.

## THE FORCE IS WITH YOU

Your values are your True North. They grow more concrete and develop with you, so even if what was True North to you at twenty-five turns out to have been just a bit more northeasterly, hopefully your values have faithfully pointed you in a generally northern direction all along the way. Thankfully, values can be cultivated beyond what nature gave you and nurture molded for you. As we think meaningfully about our values, we can shift our reference points and grow them in a more positive direction through each new experience. The values a leader holds—their definition of True North—will impact those they lead in a more direct way than their gender, age, education, or even experience.

**WHEREVER YOU LEAD, YOUR VALUES LEAD YOU**

Values held by a leader serve as the filter through which they behave and make decisions, ultimately impacting every person in their sphere of influence. These values impact the cultural dynamic of every family and organization to which they belong. Clearly defined or not, values are always present and create the undercurrent—stabilizing, reinforcing, shaping, and directing. In the context of any discussion about leadership, some determined thought surrounding values is warranted. Wherever you lead, your values lead you.

As related to leadership and as you think about your values, the question at hand remains the same. How does the foundation of your values impact your role as a leader? In your role, do you hold steadfast in the values that guide you as you lead the organization to create a bigger impact? Perhaps more importantly, are you comfortable that the path you see yourself on is consistent with how you have defined your "True North"? Positions and titles will come and go, values remain.

Values matter. They are the invisible force that drives visible results. Values should be solid. They are foundational and should not be easily persuaded or changed on a whim. But lest you think they are concrete and adopted as a set for life, let me share with you an experience I had that forever shifted my perspective on accomplishment and adjusted how I interpreted achievement. Not only that, but I became aware of the ability—the responsibility—for our values to grow as we grow and become honed with experience and time.

All it took for this awakening was for me, a Jew, to attend a graduate program at a Jesuit university ...

Chapter Six

# RE-FRAMING
## A JEW AT A JESUIT GRADUATE PROGRAM,
## LEADERSHIP ON A WHOLE OTHER LEVEL

"If you change the way you look at things,
the things you look at change."

**WAYNE DYER**
American Philosopher, Best-Selling Author

I went to work for Eddie Bauer in the mid-90s. At that time, Eddie Bauer was not a traditionally led retailer in any sense of the word, and the business culture and environment there were very new to me. It was directed by then CEO, Rick Fersch, who led in a materially and meaningfully different way. He believed in people, work-life balance, and leading from the heart. He demonstrated passion for people, for family, for work and career, and his motto could have been "doing good by and for people." This demonstrated a different kind of commitment than I had before encountered in a corporate setting. It was much more like what I had learned from my father and his perspective of honoring family while concurrently achieving his successes at the office.

Eddie Bauer merchandised in a traditional buyer and consumer format, but they went about executing this in a unique and thoroughly more enriching environment. During my tenure, I had the great fortune of being asked to attend Seattle University's graduate-level Center for Leadership. I was the first employee from Eddie Bauer to be enrolled in the program. While it was a great honor to be asked to attend the program, it was at least a little bit funny to me as well because I am Jewish and was asked to attend a Jesuit Graduate program. At thirteen I had a Bar Mitzvah and was confirmed, growing up I went to synagogue, and when I married I had a Jewish wedding. So, for Eddie Bauer to ask me to participate in a graduate program that was led by priests, pastors, and nuns from the get-go just spoke differently to me.

Well-known and respected, the Seattle University's graduate-level Center for Leadership programs was designed to challenge students to think clearly, think for themselves, and test commonly accepted knowledge. They seek to instill academic curiosity as a life-long habit.[1]

One might think I could have felt uncomfortable in the program, but there was no attempt on their part to be evangelical, but in the Jesuit tradition, they believe education is more than acquiring knowledge. What we did with that knowledge was just as important. They encouraged us to grow personally, test our values, develop responsibility for ourselves and our community, and learn to make ethical choices. They taught us to balance self-reliance with interdependence.[2] The Center for Leadership program was embedded with Jesuit teachings, though not inherently Christian.

The director of the program at the time was a nun. Dressed in street clothes (I am told the Order determines if a nun is required to wear a habit or not), but she was a nun nevertheless. This program was different in so many ways; it was not just the coursework, but even who and how it was taught. Take for instance a part of the course on ethics and morale; it was taught by a visiting professor, in fact, it was taught by the president of Gonzaga University (another Catholic institution). I was enrolled in an eight-month program, and for one of those months, I had a Catholic priest wearing a collar as my professor. Here was this president of a major university—a big school, known for their basketball team that has been in every NCAA Tournament since 1999—and their university president showed up to teach a part of our coursework on ethics and morale. Amazing.

## WHY CHOOSE ME?

In 1995 I was hired as the director of merchandising for Eddie Bauer. After my first two years, they made a change in the leadership of their home division and the vice president was asked to take on some new development separate and distinct from the home division. I was tapped to become the new Vice President of Eddie Bauer Home. This was an extension of Eddie Bauer apparel, the home division meant to appeal to the lifestyle of the person who spends time outdoors, and offer items in this category consistent with the brand. For the next two years we worked on evolving that sector of the business (which had not yet been profitable). I was to chart a course and make it profitable and was responsible to lead the entire division. I reported directly to the CEO of Eddie Bauer.

My innate abilities as a leader had only so far to go before I would run up against places where I wasn't as talented or didn't have the skills and attributes to lead further. There was room for growth in me regarding how to communicate more effectively, how to better prioritize, how to be less singularly oriented on accomplishment, and the need for me to evolve my perspective to develop a team to accomplish work.

I was the first chosen by Eddie Bauer to enroll in Seattle University's Center for Leadership program. Interestingly, this had something to do with the fact that I didn't present myself with arrogance and ego, but showed an inquisitiveness to learn, grow, and develop myself. They believed there would be interest on my part to appreciate that I had the opportunity to grow my skills and become a better leader, better partner, better collaborator ... better person. So, I was selected to formally apply.

Entrance into the program was a pretty big deal. It was designed for C-Suite leaders and to be accepted (at the time) you had to have a corporate sponsor, write essays, and have credible references among other requirements. Some of those I attended with were sponsored by Boeing, Safeco Insurance, Expeditors, and a host of other Blue Chip Fortune 100 and Fortune 500 companies. The class size was only about twenty students comprised of senior leadership people occupying real-world senior leadership roles. I felt honored to be accepted.

## THE "GREAT LOG CROSSING"

The course began with a four-day off-site immersion into the program on the shores of Lake Washington. Here we did everything from a ropes course, to team building/bonding activations. At night I remember sitting around a large firepit, lit by candles not fire, and having to share some self-effacing element of who we were, our fears and aspirations. From early on we were engaging in pretty deep sharing and a level of exposure that became foundational elements for our work together across the next eight months.

They divided the larger group into cohorts of five. I remember one exercise where there was a log and our objective was to get each member of our cohort across the log. Team one had gone and failed, they just couldn't get across. Team two had a similar approach and identical result. The third team didn't want to fail, so they spent an inordinate amount of time trying to figure out how they would accomplish the goal. We were the fourth team. I shared an idea with the team, and as a team we decided we were ready to take it on rather than wait to see the outcome of team three. We attempted to get across and did! I was given kudos for engineering our effort to cross the log instead of looking for the third team's attempt to learn from.

When it was all said and done, we had a huge debrief. The cornerstone of this was not to give great accolades for the team that crossed the log, but more to acknowledge the way we were able to get across, leapfrogging the third team. These kinds of activities were central to our learning. It was not who did or didn't do what, but instructors were constantly probing into what we learned from which leadership styles worked. They drew attention to

**THEIRS WAS A HOLISTIC APPROACH TO LEADERSHIP THAT WAS FOR AND ABOUT THE SUCCESS OF OTHERS**

how we approached taking risks. They put us through a series of physical, mental, and intellectual activities grounding us in servant-leadership, a holistic approach that was for and about the success of others, not your own. This program created an eight-month life-changing transition for me surrounding my orientation about how to lead. I learned to revel in the glory of others and not in my own individual accomplishments.

The goal of the program was for each of us to go through a process to understand the value of putting energy not into business, but leadership. Instructors presented us with many real-world business problems, and in our cohorts we focused efforts on defining what it meant to lead people; collaborating, communicating, and inspiring differently—that was the Jesuit thing. It wasn't Jesuit-driven from a religious standpoint, but it was values-driven in a way that aligned with a broad cross-section of many religions. There was a strong orientation around values, structured in how to lead more effectively given that values orientation.

For the entire eight months I melded into a series of courses, discussions, and work that was driven around holistic leadership, value-based leadership, learning to become vulnerable, take risks, and expose yourself. The program drove home a core belief that your greatest outcomes are driven by your ability to lead in a way that people want to aspire to be part of what you are leading and work at what you are doing. It was centered more on the values which work is based on rather than the work itself.

We completed assignments individually, in our cohorts, and in the full group. We wrote papers, engaged in dialogue, did mini-case studies to create plans with which we would define work against the challenges presented. Through many series of these specific real-world case-study experiences, we evolved every step of the way. Our perspectives shifted. We came out the other side not just more effective, but profoundly different leaders.

All involved in the program were also full-time executives. We didn't stop work at our companies to participate, each of us still had our primary job. Our companies would dismiss us during the workday to attend classes. Each member of the five-unit team had to write a plan, and then we would go through a process of presentation, feedback, review, and assessment. They developed our leadership and team-building skills through collaboration and addressing our perceptions. In these cohorts we learned how to cultivate dialogue and debate, entertain ideas, and tease out options developing from different points of view.

## A LASTING IMPACT

Through that program I learned what ethical leadership looked like. Today there are more courses like this, but in '99, there were few programs of this depth for this duration or having this level of impact. There was a deep emphasis on leading across a whole continuum of subjects and elements.

Those in my cohort became trusted colleagues. So much so, that until the last few years, four of us found the wherewithal to continue meeting almost monthly via teleconference or in person. A program we attended together in our youth forged a trust between us that sustained a meaningful relationship for more than twenty years. We became allies. It was incredibly valuable to have others in senior C-Suite level positions whose ethics and approach to leadership were grounded in similar values. We often met in person once a month, early in the morning. Sometimes our meetings were purely social, sometimes we worked through challenges, approaching them just as we did in our CFL cohort. Even while I was living in Dallas, I would call in to be part of the meetings, and if I were going to be in Seattle, sometimes they would make a meeting just so I could attend in person. Remaining connected with this group of people with similar values orientation and leadership perspective has proved invaluable.

There are a few others who also went through the Seattle University program with whom I still interact, though less frequently. So profound was the impact on my life that I remain on the Center for Leadership Board and meet with them every six months to help steer the program. I have spoken on their behalf either as part of a panel discussion or as an invited guest lecturer. Those eight months changed my life.

## RESHAPED

Before attending this program, I had thought about leadership in a one-dimensional way for fifteen years. Up until that point, I had been purely results-driven. This re-framing changed how I thought about, appreciated, and approached people. I began to believe the best about those I worked with, trusting that they wanted to be the best they could be. Why else would I be working with them?

I started to think about how much I loved working with someone and willingly served those whose goal in life was to help me be the best I could be and were actually capable of assisting me in becoming that. I wanted to be the best I could be. I knew if I could do that, then I could accomplish the things which were important to me. That would naturally lead to a bigger leadership role and allow me to help more people.

As I re-framed my concept of leadership, I began to listen more to what was important to those around me and became more supportive of them. I became intentional in how I could help them, more thoughtful in the ways in which I could be involved. This led to deeper, more profound relationships and was rewarding in more ways than just increased productivity. This reshaping of perspective created in me a much more overarching, outward-looking orientation.

The next generation already approaches their careers differently than how I began. They are more experiential by nature and (whether online or actual) more social, sharing their experiences. They are geared to enjoy life together and relationships hold high value with them. It isn't hard to project that as they move from their thirties into the heart of their career, many of those same relationships they value now will remain. There is more openness to the concept of mentoring than there was twenty years ago. Right now, that generation needs mentors ... and then they need to become mentors for those who will follow in their wake.

Learning to re-frame things is a valuable skill for any leader. My experience in a Jesuit university's graduate program taught me to look at things differently. That skill has continued to serve me well. "If a problem can't be solved within the frame it was conceived, the solution lies in re-framing the problem."[3]

By reshaping my definition of success and looking outward, not just defining it as "all about me" and my accomplishments, I grew. I learned I didn't have to sell my soul, but could feed it and still be successful. In the next chapter we'll explore how leaders empower the capabilities of others. I'll share how developing my own potential to lead others effectively allowed me to grow in my career and propel my progression through the ranks.

## ENDNOTES

1. Jesuit Tradition. www.seattleu.edu/jesuit-tradition/. Retrieved on 09/06/18.

2. Ibid.

3. Quote from Brian McGreevy, author and screenwriter, James Michener Fellow.

**LOOKING AT THINGS FROM A
NEW VANTAGE POINT ALLOWS
YOU TO RE-FRAME YOUR
PERSPECTIVE AND GROW**

# Chapter Seven

# ACCOMPLISHMENT
## ME AND MINE OR YOU AND YOURS, CREATING LEVERAGE TOGETHER

"Before you are a leader, success is all about growing yourself. When you become a leader, success is all about growing others."

**JACK WELCH**
Former Chairman and CEO of General Electric

Under the right leadership, people can accomplish more. Leaders accomplish more as they empower the capabilities of others. Some might even say leaders accomplish more as they do less, but I would characterize it as they "lead" vs. "tactically do." Those in higher levels of an organization are responsible for strategy. Those in lower levels in an organizational structure are responsible for the execution of that strategy—actually getting the work done.

As an individual contributor, accomplishments are largely based on completing tasks well and on time. In mid-level management roles, leaders accomplish work through others by motivating them with the vision they are trying to achieve. It is through achieving objectives that they are distinguished as they are found to be effective, efficient, and reliable. As one elevates in seniority, they will spend less and less time with their hands on daily work tasks and more time on forming a strategy. The greater their capacity to develop people, the greater their capacity to lead.

Accomplishment, then, is multiplied by developing a healthy organization that is structured by a solid plan and which harnesses the proficiencies of an empowered team. When a team of people is empowered with knowledge and guided by clear objectives, everyone accomplishes more and greater outcomes can be achieved.

## LEAD WHEREVER YOU ARE

I am writing this book at a point in my career where I have experienced some success as the CEO of a major online retailer, but I didn't start there. Part of my decision to write was from a motivation to help others who desire to do good, make a positive impact, and grow in their leadership capacity. No one starts out as a CEO, there is a progression through the ranks. This process has an element of time as well as a component of successful performance which cannot be replaced, but the equation is also dependent on one developing their own potential to lead others effectively. So, what kind of guidance is available to someone starting out at the bottom? How does one demonstrate their capability to lead if they have no one reporting directly to them?

While working for Carter Hawley Hale as an assistant buyer, I reported directly to the buyer in the junior's department. I had no one reporting to me. My job entailed a small buying responsibility within a classification, then I had the larger requirement to report to my boss and do everything that needed to be done to make our department profitable. I was in charge of no one. There was no one to whom I could delegate tasks or from whom I could harness abilities.

In the junior's department, the consumer is highly driven by trends, and therefore, fickle in their buying habits. Because trends change so rapidly, the pace is brisk. It was important to get the product out into the stores as fast as you could because one week they could want neon nylon shorts and ten days later you couldn't give neon shorts away. I was a small cog in a forty-two-store chain with a 300,000 square foot warehouse pushing out goods. I was not empowered with any authority to exercise over anyone to get them to help me achieve anything. My challenge was to lead from this place.

I took it upon myself to expedite getting the latest goods out onto the floor of my department. To that end, I would go out to the truck lines where the inbound products were received. This was in 1980, and the minimum wage was less than $3.50/hour. The guys on the line were not highly educated, they were warehouse workers loading and unloading trucks. They did not report to me, and I had nothing tangible in my power with which to motivate them to assist me. I would go visit them in the warehouse wearing my slacks and a tie and spend a bit of time with them, getting to know them personally. I was always curious about what was coming in and would say things like, "Isn't this cool?" or "Wow, this stuff is great!" while I encouraged them to get the inbound stuff onto the outbound trucks as fast as possible to help me get the goods out onto the floor. With no authority to direct them to put my boxes on the trucks first, but by showing empathy towards them and understanding what it was that motivated them, I was able to lead people who had no direct responsibility to report to me at all. These guys loved helping me and appreciated that I was engaged with them and excited about my job. They were motivated to do me a favor and get my goods on the trucks first.

This wasn't some kind of manipulation or trick. That may have worked once, but without building relationships and being able to connect meaningfully and motivate them across time, they would never have continued to consistently move my boxes first.

Most inbound goods came into the warehouse on Thursday, and through the help of these gallant warehouse warriors, I was able to have new items into the store by Friday morning and out on the floor by the same afternoon in time to entice the weekend shoppers. By closing time on Sunday evening, we often had moved about 40% of those goods.

Monday morning, I would go down to the leader of that department and thank them personally for getting the goods out so quickly. I would take them cupcakes or donuts and tell them how much we had moved and shared my genuine enthusiasm over having met goals, letting them know how important they were to me and expressing gratitude for what they had helped me to achieve. This would motivate them to repeat the performance.

They had no formal responsibility to make my department their priority. They were paid the same hourly wage regardless of how well juniors had done over the weekend. There were no bonuses for them, and no promotions were within my power to grant. It was only because I was willing to put myself in their shoes and engage with them in empathy that we built a relationship. Because I communicated my vision as well as showed appreciation for the outcomes that they helped me to create, I was able to lead them. In so doing, I could accomplish more.

## CHANGING THE DEFINITION

Throughout my career, I have been the classic "Type A" personality, driven by metrics such as bigger numbers and more significant outcomes. I think what I have accomplished thus far is because I have always pushed myself to be better than my previous self—wanting more, more, more … faster … higher … better …. I have never been, and it seems likely never will be, satisfied. I will always strive for more. I have been continuously driven to accomplish more, longed to be someplace I was not, pushed to arrive at a destination (rather than enjoying the journey), and found what I thought would be the end was just another pushing off point. I have never been comfortable or accepting of where I was, what I had accomplished, or how that stacked up. In retrospect, I note this insatiable longing and desire for more was neither materialistic nor ill-intended. Rather, it was centered around the need to do more, to be more, and to become better. I came to the conclusion that it was and still is, a continual striving for self-improvement and personal accomplishment.

While attending the Graduate Program at Seattle University, leadership began to look different than what I had come to understand. The program was organized to inspire leaders to know themselves, to lead from an ethical compass by mobilizing others around a shared vision, and seeing the connection between a better business and a better world. As previously shared, their focus provided a transformational experience that opened a path to senior leadership for me. They stimulated new ideas—not just about accomplishment, but in leading differently every day and in every way. The program helped me to begin a new chapter in my perspective of accomplishment.

It changed the context for me from "Did I win? Have I done enough? Have I been good enough as a businessman, a racer, runner, adventurer, lover ... ?" to a far more important perspective. I shifted the questions to ask, "Have I been a good enough father? Have I done well as a husband? Have I been a good friend ... and yes, as a leader too?"

It helped me to think about the critical question, "What will I leave to those I cared most about, to those who believed in me, and to our communities?"

To answer this, I had to ask additional questions that were even more important such as, "Did I give it my all? Have I lived up to my individual capacity for excellence? Have I lived up to my expectations for my own life?"

I once regarded "winning" as "everything." Accomplishment and winning were tied together in an unbreakable bond. As I shifted my perception of winning, it became defined for me as being the best I can be and being so to those who mean the most to me. Winning became treasuring the opportunity to do more, to be more, and to stretch myself in every way—to be the best that I can be. That in and of itself will be enough, I believe and is the measure by which I can feel contentment and hold myself accountable.

> **TO LIVE UP TO MY OWN INDIVIDUAL CAPACITY FOR EXCELLENCE IS ALL THE ACCOMPLISHMENT I WILL EVER NEED**

Regarding accomplishment, my reference point has shifted. It is far different today than when I was that young, ambitious man first starting out. The perspective changed, and my life's passion is now more evident to me than ever before—to live up to my own individual capacity for excellence. That is all the accomplishment I need. In this light, it became clear to me that my insatiable desire for achievement was nothing more than my expectation that I am capable of more and desire to achieve that output.

## HERE I STAND

My learning came full circle during that coursework at Seattle University. My belief that my own expectation for myself, regardless of my actual ability to achieve that level of success, also drove my expectation for others. Out of this recognition came my newfound knowledge and understanding that my own expectations to be the best were utterly tainted. I came to understand that holding myself to "my standard of "the absolute best performance" did not mean I should also hold others to the same, "my personal bar."

I realized that while some may be capable of achieving more, others might only be capable of achieving the same or less. This was a valuable insight for me. I began to use this metric to help me lead people to become the best that they could be—not my definition of best, but theirs. The "best they can be" became defined as being no more and no less than what they wanted to be. I became aware that their image of "best" might be a different standard than mine. To be the most effective of leaders then crystallized my job description: **to guide and counsel, to instill confidence and enthusiasm, to create momentum and inspiration for others in their desire to be the best they can be.**

I acknowledged that it was not likely I could raise others' innate abilities, but as a leader, I must help them to maximize the God-given talents with which they have been born. It is my job to challenge them to raise their game and inspire their desire to become the best that is within them. This is my role in leadership, in life. Through this, my passion is fulfilled and will provide me contentment for who I am and the accomplishment for which I seek.

Max Weber said, "It is immensely moving when a mature man— no matter old or young in years—is aware of the responsibility for the consequences of his conduct and feels such responsibility with heart and soul. He then acts by following an ethic of responsibility and somewhere he reaches the point where he says: 'Here I stand; I can do no other.'" I believed this. What had been important to me in the past—pure personal accomplishment, numbers, year-over-year performance, bigger jobs, more money—no longer seemed to hold the same meaning. What came to resonate with me unequivocally is delivering on what I have been blessed with and in so doing helping others to do the same. The glory in and of itself for the public glow and acknowledgment of my abilities was but a subset of a much more meaningful life and test of endurance.

> *They do not display themselves;*
> *Therefore they are illuminated.*
> *They do not define themselves;*
> *Therefore they are distinguished.*
> *They do not boast;*
> *Therefore they advance.*
> —Tao Te Ching

**To guide and counsel, to instill confidence and enthusiasm, to create momentum and inspiration for others in their desire to be the best they can be** is my aim. That is a life accomplished, a life of accomplishment!

Your view of accomplishment directly affects your ability to create successful outcomes and reach your greatest potential as a leader. Take a moment to think about how you define accomplishment. What does this mean to you?

Now with your definition of accomplishment as a key reference point, your approach to teamwork begins to take shape (or be reshaped). Your view of accomplishment frames how you will embrace diversity and even informs your thoughts on creating legacy. With our discussion of accomplishment fresh in your mind, I want to share a story with you involving my passion for cars and how curiosity leads to asking questions which opens a myriad of possibilities.

Chapter Eight

# CURIOSITY
## A LIFE-LONG ORIENTATION TO LEARNING

"I have no special talents, I am
only passionately curious."

**ALBERT EINSTEIN**
Inventor

I can relate to the curiosity of Albert Einstein and I appreciate how his attempts in developing one invention opened his mind to possibilities for other things which led to new discoveries and more inventions. I have been involved in retail in many categories and products. I jokingly say that I am a jack of all trades and master of none because I am not an expert in anything—but I do have experiences which have helped me to know a great deal about a good many different things. Some say intuition is nothing more than the summation of many experiences, and I use all these varying experiences to create a well-rounded, thoughtful perspective about the things with which I engage. I am more agile as a retailer because of my diverse experiences. This has developed my intuition and given me the ability to connect the dots and apply my understanding of the customer across all these pathways.

Though I may not be an expert in home decor, hiking gear, clothing, or jewelry, I am most certainly curious and inquisitive enough to want to learn and experience many different levels of input in any arena I have been challenged to explore. Ultimately, this steadfast belief of "I don't know what I don't know," helps better inform me as I look, listen, and learn my way through life.

There is always something more to be learned. It is wise to embrace the reality that "you don't know what you don't know," and in truth, how could you know everything? Your ability to grow is in direct correlation to your level of curiosity and inquisitiveness. Your orientation towards learning will either stretch you to expand your thinking or constrain you to live in a static world.

## DIG DEEPER

I value curiosity in those with whom I work. In an environment where people are inquisitive, I find they will ask the second and third questions, digging deeper than the surface to mine the treasures that lie beyond the obvious. A thirst for knowledge is a key ingredient necessary to arrive at a better outcome.

As an example, when I am handed a report with all the data neatly summarized for me, I do not focus on that summary and take action based solely on that data. The summary, of course, is efficient and expected. It is not that I don't trust the report or the person who created it, but it is not my inclination to just take the bottom number and run with it.

Being curious and inquisitive, I look at the data, scan the input, do some quick mental math, and evaluate the summary. I ask, "What does the data mean?" In reviewing the report, I am thinking through the raw data, possessing both the experience and the intuition to access the report in real time while asking myself additional questions. Even if everything about a report seems to check out at face value, my curiosity causes me to engage the one presenting the report in dialogue around the summary.

If something does not make sense intellectually or intuitively, in that relatively quick assessment, I go hunting. I search for data or words that are not congruent, looking to spot a metric that seems like it may be wrong. If I do see something that unravels the work, I dig deeper and really begin to look at all the elements, seeking to better understand if there is something erroneous with the formula or in the data itself. I ask if it could be interpreted in another way. I am always searching for the answers to questions like: How did we get here? Why is this right? What are the input levers that created this outcome?

By digging deeper and having the disposition to ask the second and third questions, I get a better outcome. This curiosity is not born from trying to catch someone out or challenge the quality of their work but instead stems from a desire to learn, to grow, and to explore. It has served me well. I am a life-long student, always eager to learn and explore new possibilities. Curiosity has become a discipline for how I think and act.

**HAVING THE CURIOSITY TO ASK THE SECOND AND THIRD QUESTIONS LEADS TO BETTER OUTCOMES**

Ask a lot of questions. Surround yourself with curious and inquisitive people who also ask a lot of questions. If you are surrounded only by people who already know it all, they don't need to ask anything—and they are usually set on telling you what to do! I am most certainly not an expert at most anything, but I have learned that looking for insights, learning, and exploring will pay me back in triplicate as that new knowledge helps me navigate in ways I never imagined before.

# CURIOSITY COULD SAVE THE CAT

I love cars. I own a fifty-year-old English sports car and it is exhilarating to drive. I recently took it to my mechanic because the overdrive was working intermittently. On the phone the owner told me, "Oh, it's probably just the mechanism sliding and not holding when you put it into overdrive, it's about a fifteen-minute fix."

This was his experience talking. He is a highly regarded mechanic and owns a business built on restoring foreign (British) automobiles. He knows his stuff! But after twenty-five minutes of checking under the hood he said to me, "Hmm, it's not what I thought,"  and he put the car up on a lift to perform an electrical diagnosis of the system. Based on his experience and intuition and because of the system diagnosis, he uncovered what he believed to be the problem—a bad solenoid. Because it is a fifty-year-old sports car, and the part cannot be accessed from the engine to replace, he told me they would have to take the car apart, fix it, then put it all back together.

An hour and a half later, they had removed the carpet and taken out the seats … all to get to the tiny part that needed to be replaced. At last, they were finished. He tested the solenoid only to discover it was perfectly fine. After all that effort and time, he determined that was not the issue after all. We were nowhere. The problem remained.

Just then, a younger mechanic came in—a curious mechanic with a passion for cars. After a few minutes of investigation he said to the owner, "I don't know why you started there, have you tested this?" and he pointed to something under the hood.

"No," the older mechanic shrugged, his experience telling him that probably wasn't the answer, "but we can."

There inside the engine compartment bolted onto the firewall is a relay switch. This relays the current from the solenoid out, causing the overdrive to respond. As it turns out, the relay was the part that was bad. Two bolts, a new relay, and the job was done.

The new mechanic had not known what the problem was. He has a great deal less experience than the seasoned owner, and this interest in other options caused him to ask a few questions. The veteran mechanic had not identified what the issue was but had drawn his conclusions from previous experience. He had not gone any further exploring other possibilities in his mind. He did not ask himself the second and third questions before committing energy and time. The less experienced mechanic had walked in midstream and knew only that the solenoid wasn't the problem, so he investigated other options. Had they done that, to begin with, the whole process actually would have taken only fifteen minutes, and there would have been no need to go the long (and unnecessary) route of taking the car apart.

How often do we allow our knowledge and experience to put us on auto-pilot and become close-minded to understanding more options—better options? The close-ended view is rarely as brilliant as the one which is open to curiosity. By being willing to ask more questions and look at things from multiple perspectives, you can access a myriad of possibilities.

**THE CLOSE-ENDED VIEW IS RARELY AS BRILLIANT AS THE ONE WHICH IS OPEN TO CURIOSITY**

# HELP THEM GET THERE ON THEIR OWN

In the development of any relationship, I like to begin with open-ended questions. By asking questions that encourage dialogue, I can begin to understand how a person thinks, recognize their level of depth, appreciate their areas of expertise, and identify how they arrive at an outcome. With this as a foundation, as the relationship grows I have confidence that when they bring me answers they have been thoughtful.

Conversely, if I encounter someone who cannot provide any substantive reason for doing something and their answers are largely opinion-based or have no demonstrative analytical perspective or data driving them, I am less confident about outcomes they present. As a leader, I seek to help them grow in curiosity. Rather than accepting or rejecting their answers, I will ask more questions, but these are now more close-ended, attempting to stimulate their curiosity and thus, help them get there on their own. My hope is that they will have a realization and arrive at the understanding that they haven't yet dug deep enough, that their answer is not thoughtful, and therefore, their analysis might not be correct.

If that light still doesn't go off for them, then I become more directive and author a point of view. Because it is not my aim to belittle or deride, I don't say, "You're wrong." Instead, I would be more inclined to offer something like, "It's not that I am saying you are wrong, but I don't understand this. This math doesn't work," or "The basis with which you have offered your perspective doesn't make sense to me, and here is why." In this way, I can address an issue or concern without making the person feel defensive.

If we still aren't there, I obviously cannot act on their outcome. At that point, it is time to step in and to engage with them in dialogue, but specifically, from my perspective and in a more directed manner. Even at this stage, it is my goal to remain respectful. Perhaps they are right, but

I didn't know or understand something. I don't start out saying, "You're an idiot, this is wrong." That would only cause them to push back and suddenly, we are totally off track. By giving them the opportunity, "Help me understand. The way your algorithm works doesn't make sense to me," I still try to get them to question their formula on their own and get to an if/then outcome. In trying to help me understand why it is right or wrong, hopefully, they will arrive at their own conclusion along the way.

While this takes time and I could just point out what I think I see as wrong, the dividend is that the person will have gotten there on their own and in reality, what if I just have misread what I thought. Hopefully, the next time they bring me a report they will have pushed their data through their own series of questions and be ready to make a case for their numbers before presenting. Allowing them to get there on their own empowers them for the future.

## LET'S MAKE A (BETTER) DEAL

Whenever you negotiate anything, inherently you are negotiating to what you want to make happen. Someone on the other side is bargaining to get to what they want to make happen and it is a place different than where you are seeking to arrive, hence the negotiation. If I go into that negotiation and act as if I know nothing and play dumb (even though I may not be) I have the opportunity to ask a lot of questions. I can use those questions to create a better outcome.

I can ask objective questions from the premise of "I don't know, I am asking to learn." I can also ask questions that challenge specific perspectives on a contract, on pricing, delivery, or whatever. If I am too directive and dig in my heels, then I am negotiating to a point that they are negotiating against. I know that somewhere in the middle something will happen. In the middle ground, I am still trying to get them to a place where I want them to be, but the approach is more disarming. To the degree that I can lead them to a path they can arrive at on their own without telling them what that is, they will be more pleased with the conclusion.

In negotiating, asking questions may be less about actually being curious than it is about presenting an inquisitiveness that will aid you in getting the outcome you want. Through asking questions, your case is presented in a way that is disarming and allows them to arrive at a favorable finish. Rather than feeling like they lost a negotiation, that party instead feels like they got to a good position.

There is an art to it, to be sure. Being a Type-A person and enjoying the surge of competition, I must be careful about pacing. I have to keep myself in check during the process. I can go too far too fast and exhibit too much intensity. If questions feel like an inquisition, the other party will become defensive. If they are not thoughtful enough, they can feel insulted or irritated. Having self-awareness regarding the questions asked and possessing the ability to pace myself to allow the conclusions to happen easily instead of being in a hurry-up mode and pushing them too fast is key. Curiosity is definitely a beneficial tool in the art of negotiation and in reality, it is a genuine curiosity as it typically helps get to a better place.

## BEING COMFORTABLE BEING UNCOMFORTABLE

By now you know that being comfortable being uncomfortable is a theme for me. As one goes up the ladder, it can be really uncomfortable to risk looking silly by asking what might be perceived as a dumb question. Exposing a lack of knowledge is uncomfortable with many people. In high-level leadership, there is a balance between appearing curious or asking so many questions people would challenge your competence. Sometimes in the heat of battle, I find myself asking a question and immediately think, "If I had been more thoughtful, I probably could have gotten there without asking." If I *should* know something and ask the question anyway, it can look bad, but I am comfortable being uncomfortable. I am secure in my own skin and being curious is important to me as a personal core trait.

I have found that the curiosity of leaders actually raises the level of employee engagement. People love when you are interested in them. The investment of getting to know employees pays huge dividends. Your curiosity as a leader is up front and on center stage when you take the time to find out what is important to them. Ask questions about them, ask about their kids, find out what their career aspirations are, what challenges they are facing, and everything in between. To the extent you know them and are genuinely interested in them, trust is built. In that process of asking questions, you are teaching them how to be an effective partner, leader, manager ... Curiosity propels the building of relationships and gives you insight into those who work for you. They gain the perspective on how what they are working on will enhance the total outcome. Curiosity leads to high engagement, and a highly engaged workforce is enthusiastic.

If those you lead see that you are comfortable being uncomfortable, then they can risk being uncomfortable too. They can risk being curious which instills confidence and enthusiasm. Curiosity helps to create momentum and inspiration for others in their desire to be the best they can be.

Curious people are almost never arrogant. They never represent themselves as knowing it all. Rather, their curiosity is an expression of things they do not yet know and would like to learn. Though you will not likely find it in any psychology textbook, I see a link between curiosity and humility in a leader. Not limited to a focus on what is new, curiosity also values what has been and why it worked and how it could be made better. Humble leaders create and drive a culture around a desire to learn, to explore. In this, their curiosity is a key indicator of their humility. In the next chapter, I'll tell you about a time when I was challenged to appreciate the way things were while navigating necessary major change to help a floundering company survive, and ultimately, thrive.

Chapter Nine

# HUMILITY
## ARROGANCE IS SO UNATTRACTIVE, CONFIDENCE CAN BE CAPTIVATING

"Humility must accompany all our actions,
must be with us everywhere; for as soon as
we glory in our good works they are of no
further value to our advancement in virtue."

**ST. AUGUSTINE OF HIPPO**
Fourth Century Philosopher, Roman African Theologian

Aconfident leader is one who recognizes the best qualities in others
without being threatened. With an easy awareness of their authority
and capabilities, they are sure in their decisions and actions, but also aware
and appreciative of the views of others. They see people as valuable and
worthy of notice, their gifts and skills worthy of exploration. Whatever
a situation calls for, a confident leader exhibits a calm control of their
own abilities. While secure in their qualifications and experience, they
are also aware they do not know it all, and demonstrate a commitment
to learn all they can.

Between confidence and arrogance, you will not find a fine line, but rather a large gap. An arrogant person asks no questions for which they do not already have an answer. They will present themselves as being the smartest in the room and voice a strong opinion without considering the impact of that opinion. Steamrolling ideas over others is not the same thing as sticking to your guns. In fact, aggression in a leader often indicates a low-level of confidence which masks itself as bravado and comes across as audacity, not confidence.

An arrogant person will not embrace vulnerability, for them it is weakness. Uncertainty is viewed as a threat, and therefore, risks will not be taken unless blame can be shifted in the event a result does not pan out. By being unwilling to learn what they do not already know, an arrogant person limits their potential for growth. Sadly, it isn't only themselves they constrain—brilliant ideas from others on the team go unheard, curiosity is squashed, and innovation is not permitted to see the light of day.

Confident leaders have no need to bully anyone to see their goals accomplished and can share the oxygen in the room with others. They are solid in their point of view, but they have no need to push that point of view on top of others. People equate their calm confidence with competence, and therefore, trust their leadership. We like to work with people we can believe in. We tend to believe in people who genuinely believe in themselves. When you are confident in your beliefs and have conviction regarding your point of view, it comforts those who look to you for guidance. When you are sure of your abilities and demonstrate a willingness to both grow in those abilities and embrace the abilities of others, people know they can count on you. When you articulate a point of view that is backed by years of experience and credible insights, even if you are in uncharted waters or in an unsteady moment, people will give you the benefit of the doubt. Each time you prove yourself worthy of trust, their confidence in you grows and your self-confidence is reinforced.

As surely as anxiety and fear are contagious, confidence also projects itself to others, but in a positive way. When there is confidence in the atmosphere, there is room for people to challenge ideas in a constructive, respectful manner that is not driven by a need to be right, but rather by the desire to do things the right way. A confident leader never forgets where they came from or takes themselves too seriously. Instead, their confidence is based in the ability to harness the abilities of others. They know success is never the result of a solitary effort, but from a group's contribution.

## WHAT'S IN YOUR WAKE?

If you have ever paid attention to a boat on a lake, you've noticed it creates a wake behind it as it cuts through the water. If the boat is moving, it will leave a wake of some sort. In much the same way, a leader creates a wake behind them through their actions and conversations. A vortex is created behind a leader that draws things toward it. The accepted practices and taboos of an organization—good or bad—all stem from that leadership. The wake behind a leader is the culture that leader is creating for that organization to operate within. If a leader asks questions and engages people, if they listen, learn, and are empathetic; then those who follow are inspired to work with and for them. At the opposite end of the spectrum, an autocratic or dictatorial leader creates a vortex of chaos and distrust around them. Those caught in their wake do everything they can to pull themselves out, like a swimmer trying to escape a dangerous undertow before they drown!

## RESPECT WHAT WAS TO CHANGE WHAT IS

Moosejaw opened their first store in 1992 in Keego Harbor, Michigan, and in 1995 they ventured into the world of online retail. For a glimpse of the quirky, fun culture known as "Moosejaw Madness," you can visit their website and find as part of their story: "1996—We copied all our marketing ideas from Shirley's Stuffed Cat Shop. Fortunately, Shirley died shortly after filing a lawsuit."[1] This is typical of their humor.

An incredible organization, Moosejaw developed a cult-like consumer following around the founder's vision for how to "Engagingly Engage" their customers. The business was not built around selling proprietary goods, instead they sell well-recognized brands like The North Face®, Patagonia®, Black Diamond™, and others. Because the brands sold are available in many retail outlets, they had to create something special to get people to shop with them—and they did. Their secret sauce is not in what they sell, but how they sell it.

They have a way of making customers feel like part of a club that has a secret handshake. You feel like an insider when you buy from them. If you visit a retail store, you might walk into an all-out Nerf® gun battle among the employees and get hit with a foam bullet while shopping. But don't worry, they have guns for you too, so you can play along. If you purchase a down jacket from their online store, instead of a boring FedEx® box arriving at your door, Moosejaw sends it out wrapped in their proprietary white packaging with red letters and the iconic red antlers. On the package you'll find the instruction: "NO KNIFE. USE TEETH." Of course, this makes people laugh and represents the unorthodox, fun, quirky Moosejaw customer, but it is actually a tongue-in-cheek practical instruction. As it turns out, people had been opening their boxes with a knife and would accidentally slice into their new down jackets, damaging them. The solution was branding genius! If you happen to spot a Moosejaw delivery truck, on the back you will see in large letters, "Driver carries less than $50 cash and is fully naked." While an obvious exaggeration, it makes you chuckle while delivering the message: nothing to steal here.

The unique customer experience they created allowed them to thrive in a time when many .com businesses had come and gone. Their disruptive approach yielded a steady increase of sales and profitability through their online and brick and mortar presence across a respectable 17 years.

Profits grew into the multi-millions, and by 2006 the company had been named Best of The Web by Forbes magazine, listed as a Top 50 Retailer by Internet Retailer and Bizrate, and they were also recognized by the New York Times as a leader in online marketing.[2] In 2007 a Dallas-based private equity firm acquired a stake in the company just as the economy was hit by the mortgage and banking crisis. In 2008, every company had to adjust their understanding of business and adapt quickly to the economic climate regarding product assortment, logistics, supply chains, and marketing to consumers. Companies everywhere were undergoing major financial stress, and it was true survival of the fittest.

Moosejaw's incredible growth came to a standstill. Then still became stop and stop became reverse as sales plummeted. In a year-over-year comparison, profitability declined so rapidly, that what had been multi-million dollar profits turned into multi-million dollar losses. That's when I joined the team.

The challenge was to find ways to keep the leading edge in customer engagement, but with a plan that better understood the challenges of the new economy and how to navigate the business with the process, structure, and discipline required in those uncertain times. They had tried a number of things that just had not worked out, and it was time to craft a solid plan.

It was not easy. The staff was uneasy and finances were in dire straits. My challenge was to appreciate, understand, and respect the culture by mining what had already been created, fully engaging the employee population and maintaining consumer engagement. I practiced listen, look, and learn to find ways to extend that secret sauce in a way that made sense in the new economic climate. I needed to know what worked and what didn't work to create a course for recovery. Where something was working, we needed to drive deeper into those categories, create marketing initiatives, and find ways to reduce expenses and streamline logistics all without losing the incredible culture and environment created through the leadership and vision of the founder. If we lost that, we would quickly become just another retailer selling someone else's products.

When I joined the team, we were bleeding cash. It was incredibly challenging on so many levels, and I was alert to how employees perceived this new CEO coming in from Dallas, "What does he know? Can he help us?" Every decision made had an impact on the balance sheet. We undertook the very difficult decisions to lay-off some of the staff, cut expenses, become lean and mean, and do whatever it was going to take to create breathing room. We worked with our supplier partners to address payables, deferred expenses, and through it all, became a team dedicated to seeing the tough times through.

In the first six months I was there, we were literally fighting for our lives. I spent most of those early months trying to understand the culture, make payroll, and find ways how best to leverage this incredible team with a plan; then establish the process, structure, and discipline to execute that strategic plan and to move forward. The company had to absorb a new leader, and they had to be confident that leader understood all the elements. I could not be arrogant, but needed to proceed with the confidence to inspire the team as well as humility, this motivated me to exhibit great awareness for how I showed up to accomplish that.

This confident humility was demonstrated through my serious appreciation for the special reasons Moosejaw was unique. I had the confidence to believe I could bring them to a new level of discipline without destroying what made them exceptional.

I wrote a 100-day plan, fully aware of my team's concerns, crafted through open dialogue, and engaging employees from customer care to warehouse staff to in-store people. When I first introduced it, I chose what may have seemed to be an almost juvenile approach—I made a PowerPoint illustration to help them understand who Harvey Kanter was and why I was relevant as a leader in this place. I literally put together photos of my younger days as a backpacker and mountain climber. There were photos of me on the summit of Mt. Rainier and backpacking on the Pacific Ocean seashore in Washington State. I communicated

my appreciation openly for the category of products we sold and that I could relate to it. I knew my decisions would not resonate with everybody, but they put us on a path to return to profitability. The second half of the year took off—sales grew, profit came back, and by year-end the world looked a lot different.

There was no magic formula, no silver bullet. My confidence in the company and steady belief that things could and would turn around set the tone for the come-back. As an organization, we believed, the course was set, and we grabbed onto the vision. We built a strategic and tactical operating plan which was executed with unwavering fortitude. Because we believed in each other and in what we were doing, we persevered. It was not really sexy (the plan); it was blocking and tackling, assortment planning, developing a go-to-market calendar, driving consumer engagement, marketing … and it was execution.

I relished the experience. For three and a half years I commuted from Dallas to Detroit, living out of a hotel room and riding a bike twelve miles to the office each day (yes, in very cold weather too)! When I left the company, my successor was one of my senior managers, and we were able to present to the board a viable succession plan. Today Moosejaw is still around and has gone on to even better times and experienced monumental growth.[3] Confidence and humility had its reward.

# SERVANT-LEADERSHIP EQUATION

Each quality discussed should not be considered as stand-alone ingredient—add one cup confidence to two cups accountability. It doesn't work like that. But to some degree, I believe you will find a blend of each of these characteristics in every good leader. How those ingredients blend together and in what proportions are what makes each person and their leadership style unique. Humility is an important element of leadership in how it informs communication, optimism, tenacity ... and all the other qualities of a leader.

The job of a leader is to knock out of the way things that are blocking the path, to reduce friction, to increase collaborative efforts, create a unified vision, and to support people. If no one works with you, who are you leading? Your job is not to get people to do things for your benefit, but to do things for their benefit. Leaders serve the people, no matter what job they are performing. Effective leaders understand how to support people and serve them to achieve the outcomes you are driving and asking them to drive.

So, what role does humility play in this function of a leader? How does humility serve **to guide and counsel, to instill confidence and enthusiasm, to create momentum and inspiration for others in their desire to be the best they can be.** If leadership is ultimately about serving, then the servant-leadership model is rooted in the knowledge that neither authority nor hierarchy will help create an appetite for growth. Humble leaders create and drive a culture around a desire to learn, to explore. The humility of a leader shows their vulnerability, their willingness to be curious in all the things. This confidence inspires others to be learners as well; to push, take risks, and "go where no man has gone before." Your example encourages those who follow you to try new things and learn along the way, mistakes and all. A key element in the character of a leader, humility encourages others to step up and step out.

Humility recognizes there is always a better self trying to emerge and will push through challenges in order to grow. Mother Teresa said, "If you are humble nothing will touch you, neither praise nor disgrace, because you know what you are." A humble leader knows things will not always go well, but by persevering through adversity, you develop that important quality of resilience we discussed earlier. While it takes humility to endure failure without letting it crush you, it takes tenacity to try again when you miss the mark. In the next chapter we'll talk about tenacity and I'll share a story about another one of my great passions, running, which illustrates the power of perseverance. Leaders never quit. Let's talk next about how leaders develop the endurance to stick it out.

## ENDNOTES

1. *About Moosejaw*. www.moosejaw.com/madness/about. Retrieved from the web 08/31/2018.

2. *Moosejaw: How the Support Team Uses Playback Sessions to "Engagingly Engage" With Customers*. www.fullstory.com/customers/moosejaw/. Retrieved from the web 08/31/18.

3. 2017—I thought I lost my favorite hat but then I found it. That's about it. Oh, plus we went through monumental growth. But man, I'm glad I found that hat. https://www.moosejaw.com/madness/about. Retrieved from the web 09/06/2018.

HUMBLE LEADERS CREATE AND DRIVE A
CULTURE AROUND A DESIRE TO LEARN AND
EXPLORE, THIS INSPIRES OTHERS TO PUSH,
TAKE RISKS, STEP UP, AND STEP OUT

Chapter Ten

# TENACITY
## IF YOU THINK YOU CAN, YOU WILL

"We will either find a way or make one."
**HANNIBAL**
(247-182 BC) Carthaginian General

Life is a marathon, not a sprint. This is an overused cliché, but clichés are born from the reality of circumstance and experience. Endurance, tenacity, and perseverance are required of those who want to go the distance and finish well. Perseverance is a core trait present in all great leaders, it allows them to keep going when times get tough. Their tenacity keeps everyone else going too—all the way to the goal. They appreciate the opportunities that are accessed only along the difficult path and know that potential and perseverance are linked.

In an earlier chapter, I shared that I have always pushed myself to be better than my previous self—always striving for more, continuously driven to accomplish more. Whatever I think will be an end is just another pushing off point. That's because success is not something at which you ever arrive. Progress requires moving forward, seizing new opportunities and all the challenges that come with them. Having the ability to persevere when things are not going well is something I value in others and goad myself along. How do you deal with adversity? Can you claw your way through a trying time? Tenacity creates a certain resiliency that keeps you pushing towards vision, come what may.

Since my college days I had been an on-again, off-again, recreational runner. When I moved to Chicago back in 1993, my then neighbor, an avid runner, began urging me to run with him over and over. I took him up on it, and from that point I considered myself to be a "casual runner," (though not a "serious runner"). Some days I would run with my neighbor, but often enough I ran on my own—with no music—just me, myself and I. My work life was pretty intense. Add to that raising the two kids we had at the time (with one on the way) and all the things that go with life, and running provided quality time for me to be alone and process my thoughts, reflect about life and family, work and strategy. I grew to love this almost meditative time alone. It was good for both my physical and mental health. On a rare occasion I might extend my run to 7 miles, but in reality, I was a 3–5-mile guy.

By 1999, my occasional 3–5 miles became a regular 5–7 miles, most often at 5 a.m. I loved the quiet time, the incredible wakening of each day in this way. The Sunday before Thanksgiving, a friend asked me to run the Seattle Marathon with him. Full of bravado and confidence I said, "Sure! Why not? What the heck!" and the following week, I ran a marathon. I went from running 20–25 miles in a week to running 26 miles at one stretch. Physically, it wasn't all that bad. I was fine, though admittedly I could not walk up any stairs for the next two days, but it was all good. The run was more about mental fortitude. It was about tenacity and perseverance. (Posting a time of 4:01 to complete the marathon was not bad either!) It was about why not, not why. For me, at least, it was about experiencing great challenge—physical and mental—to offset and test myself against the relatively easy life we have, with nearly anything we want at a hand's length access.

## "I CAN, SIR" NOT CANCER

Running played an important role in my fight against cancer. I ran every single day, no matter how tired I felt from treatments. My 5–7 miles averaging 7.5 minutes per mile or so eventually dwindled down

to 2–3 miles per day and about 12 minutes per mile, but I never conceded. My assistant had a running t-shirt made for me that had the words "Optimism" and "Fortitude" on the front, "Perseverance" on the sleeves, and "Tenacity" emblazoned across the back. No matter how sick I was, I ran every day in that shirt. I have since given that shirt to two of my friends who have also been stricken with cancer, and both times when their treatments were done they mailed it back.

This shirt has come to represent hope and optimism. It has become a standard. Persevere. Fight. Win.

Post-cancer I kept thinking, *Can I give back? Can I make a difference? Make an impact?* Honestly, I wanted to find ways to acknowledge how thankful I was to be alive and still standing tall. What better way than to train for and run another marathon? I had not trained for my last marathon and did pretty well. I thought if I trained, then perhaps I could qualify for the Boston marathon. It seemed like a smart idea.

In the spring of 2008, I began looking for a marathon to run that was as close as possible to the date of my original cancer diagnosis. I decided I would raise money for the cause by running. I looked for a cancer organization that either helped those stricken with cancer in treatment or in finding cures. I told a very good friend, John Colocousis, about my plan and he said, "That sounds like an incredible journey. Mind if I run and raise funds with you?"

So together we trained. John was an avid marathoner and had finished many, while I had but one to my record (and that was on a whim). I made an assumption that training with him would do me wonders. As often happens, the plan did not go as smoothly as I envisioned. We signed up for Livestrong, the charity, and trained hard. We came across

"The Skagit Valley Marathon" in Washington State scheduled for September 7, 2008. Both my friend and I lived in Dallas, but we agreed this was the right event, so we committed to be there and began training. I had some chronic back pain issues, but the challenges came and went, so I pressed through them.

The marathon approached. The day before the race, we flew from Dallas to Seattle, drove two hours to Skagit, registered to run, and hydrated. All 248 runners were ready. Yep, you read that correctly, 248 runners! The course was 13 miles out and back. It was hard to find enough volunteers to tend to the needs of 248 runners, and it was a Boston qualifying marathon to boot! I finished, but it was not pretty. My back went south early in the day. Training with my friend did not work out as well as I had hoped, and in the end, I ran the marathon and finished about 10 minutes SLOWER than my first marathon (which I never really trained for). That said, between John and me we raised nearly $45,000 for Livestrong. We flew home on the red-eye that night, and in spite of my slower time of 4:11, we felt pretty good about the accomplishment of finishing and raising funds for a good cause.

## LET'S GO AGAIN!

If at first you fail to succeed, try, try again. We had done pretty well with the fundraising, so I decided to do it again. This time around I would shoot for raising the same amount of money, but perhaps change up the training, not injure myself along the way, and take another shot at running a sub-four hour marathon. The New York City Marathon was only about a month past my second-anniversary date, so on that second anniversary of being cancer free, I decided I would try again.

November 7, 2009 was meant to be my "sub-4 hour" marathon. By this time, I was living in Detroit during the week at the helm of Moosejaw and commuting back to Dallas each weekend. This was not ideal for training, and I didn't have John to partner with except on weekends, so I just persevered on my own. I want to say another day, another dollar … or maybe another step, another mile, but it really did not go that way. While I did run, train, and make the most of the pre-marathon time to get ready, it did not work out so well.

Getting older is just no fun. My body was not recovering as I wanted it to. I trained. I did yoga for three months to strengthen my back and saw a few professionals along the way, trying to keep it together. My back doctor prescribed some medication to help with inflammation and spasms. I took these intermittently as needed, but trudged ahead, preparing for the big day. On my last training run, I ran nearly 26 miles, but it wasn't pretty. I hoped I was ready. I was as ready as I was going to be.

The day dawned cold and windy. It was more blustery than it had been for any NYC Marathon in some time. This go around, not only did John Colocousis join me, but Bryan Lively and Alison Norton did as well. The four of us made up "Team Cancer Sucks" and once again,

we ran for Livestrong. With great excitement we arrived at the starting line at 6:00 a.m. We agreed we would run together for the first mile, but John had a great training regiment, as did Cous (Bryan) as he was known, so we knew they would quickly outpace Alison and me. We were each committed to finish strong.

I ran okay for the first 7–8 miles, but by mile 9, I was in trouble. I was already experiencing pain and spasms in my back. I persevered for a bit, but it became (painfully) obvious I was in trouble. I had the presence (or stupidity) of mind to bring along the remaining prescription for pain and spasms, and with the help of these at about mile 14, I did plod through. The highlight was my bride waiting there for me at mile 16 as I came across the 61st Street Bridge and circled the cloverleaf as it came around. I am not even sure how I could have seen her with the 100,000 people who were there at that point in the run. It was schizophrenic and chaotic, but with all those people cheering the runners, equally as energizing. Somehow in spite of the thousands of people, I saw my wife! She kissed me and on I went. At about mile 22 I again saw her again as I began to enter Central Park and she willed me to go on. Let's just say it was NOT the sub-4 hour run I had hoped for. In fact, it was 4:26—even slower than Skagit Valley, but I did finish. I persevered and I finished. Later that night, the four of us and our spouses celebrated together. We raised nearly $50,000 and had made a difference.

## MIND OVER MATTER PUSH BACK, PRESS ON

The story isn't really about finishing the race. It isn't even about raising money or doing good, though these things are all really important. The story illustrates the power of perseverance. It demonstrates that you can do nearly anything you put your mind to. It would have been easy enough to quit that day. No one would have thought any less of me for yielding to the pain in my body and sitting out the remainder of the race. I could have stopped at any point and the pain would have eased, but I would have regretted that decision the moment I made it. I would have walked if I had to, crawled even, but I was determined I would persevere to the end. I pushed through the wall to fulfill my commitment. I wanted to make a difference, not an exit. Together, the four of us made an impact, and in some small way, hopefully helped make life a bit easier for those stricken with cancer or fighting to find cures.

When I battled cancer, my tenacity gave me the ability to push back in my own mind. I could look at all the facts and still say, "I will win. Cancer won't." Pushing myself to run while I was sick helped me persevere. In the beginning, I didn't know if the cancer would come back in a year or two years … or never. So I celebrate each anniversary trying to raise funds for the cause. I started by running those marathons to raise money, and now for four years in a row I have been riding a bike in charity events in Seattle and across six events, I have been able to raise almost $500k.

I'm very active in my fundraising, I'm even okay with calling and emailing all my friends and killing them with requests for funds. I preface these appeals with, "I'm sorry if I am making you crazy, but we are curing cancer here—it's literally a matter of life and death." My passion for this cause is backed up by what I am willing to sacrifice for it. That kind of perseverance pays off.

## TRUE GRIT

The Latin root for the word tenacity is "*tenax*" which means "holding fast." Leaders hold fast to vision. They hold fast to goals and ideals. Good leaders hold fast to their values. The world transforms more quickly than at any period ever before in the history of man. The pace of change has grown too rapid for most to even keep up, there is unprecedented uncertainty. It is in this climate that leaders must hold fast. They must demonstrate the character to sustain commitment in tough, tumultuous times. This quality of tenacity instills confidence in those who look to you for guidance and inspiration. They know you won't give up, so they won't either. When you push to be the best you can be, you encourage others to do the same.

Dr. Travis Bradberry said, "Grit is that 'extra something' that separates the most successful people from the rest. It's the passion, perseverance, and stamina that we must channel in order to stick with our dreams until they become a reality." Don't be too quick to jump ship or throw in the towel. Find a way to push through the challenges. Develop relentless persistence. Endure the punches and never leave the ring. When perseverance is added to passion, great things are possible.

Tenacity, however, should never be confused with stubbornness. Enduring adversity and persevering through challenges is not the same as holding to an outdated method of doing things or clinging to old ways of thinking when challenged by fresh thought. Therefore, in our discussion of tenacity and all its merits, it is relevant to bring up the subject of diversity, and consider how mindsets and strategies to overcome obstacles must also be applied to embracing new approaches. Staying on task need not be in opposition to learning and growing.

In the next chapter we'll talk about diversity, dialogue, and debate. Tenacity definitely plays a role in the process of leveraging diverse ideas, opinions, and the experiences of a whole team. I'll tell you a story about a time when innovation of thought from new, younger leaders challenged the stability of long-engrained ideas and a time-tested approach. I'll share about the process involved to create a plan, manage the risks, and successfully implement a new strategy.

**LEADERS MUST DEMONSTRATE
THE CHARACTER TO SUSTAIN
COMMITMENT IN TOUGH,
TUMULTUOUS TIMES**

## Chapter Eleven

# DIVERSITY
## DIALOGUE, DEBATE, AND DIFFERENT POINTS OF VIEW

"Diversity: the art of thinking
independently together."

**MALCOLM FORBES**
Publisher of Forbes Magazine

In any good conversation among great people, there is bound to be differing perspectives, opinions, and ideas. This is healthy. The diversity available from connecting with the intellect and experiences of others from lives well led is profound. It requires a certain maturity to appreciate a range of thoughts, acknowledge there are multiple points of view, and engage in rich dialogue and debate. This practice leads to gaining greater insights and innovation of thought and enriches any culture where it is encouraged to thrive.

This is exactly what the world needs—debate, discussion, and dialogue. True, if we all thought alike we may be more zen-like, awash in a sea of melancholy, but it is unlikely we would advance through curiosity and innovation. The exploration of disruptive technologies in the Twenty-First Century has created the humanity we know today as well as the one we have yet to discover. Why? Because people dare to think differently (a respectful head nod to Mr. Jobs is appropriate here). They dare to challenge the borders and boundaries of conventional approaches, they refuse to accept the limitations of the status quo, and they are changing everything.

## BACK TO THE FUTURE

"The Jetsons" aired its debut episode on television in September 1962.[1] While many readers were likely not even alive and won't know of the show, its use of flying cars, video chats, robotics, holograms and 3-D printing back in '62 were as far-fetched as you could ever imagine. Like much of America, I enjoyed watching many episodes of "The Jetsons," in syndication in the 70s and have fond memories of the Jetson family living in a utopian, modernistic future where people lived in houses in the sky, worked three-day workweeks, drove aero-cars that looked like flying saucers, and had so many conveniences that there was plenty of time for leisure. George lived in the Skypad Apartments with his homemaker wife, Jane, and their children, Judy and Elroy. The house was tended by their robotic maid, Rosie, and they had a talking dog named Astro.

It has been more than fifty years since the cartoon was created, but the technology that came to life in animation five decades ago is still equating to real-world breakthroughs we are now using today: treadmills, moving sidewalks, jetpacks, and video calls to name a few. The show represented the future, and impacted many of those who were kids back then, but are presently our social, business, and political leaders.[2]

The original show lasted for just one season, 24 episodes, but the replays of those shows were so popular that the series had a resurrection in the 1980s, producing more episodes for syndication.[3] A child's cartoon, this narrative has deeply impacted society and pushed exploration into the possibilities of technology. In reality, we are not yet there, but electric, self-driving cars are no longer a fad, they are a mode of travel firmly embedded into daily life. Electric bikes are everywhere, bird scooters are multiplying like guppies, hoverboards can be picked up at your local Wal-Mart, and flying cars are not far behind. We are well on our way to having a taste of the life George and Judy Jetson lived. Back in the 60s, this was science fiction, fanciful imagination. Today it represents the diversity of thought from people like Steve Jobs, Elon Musk, Jeff Bezos and others—the modern-day incarnations of past disruptive innovators like Christopher Columbus, Thomas Edison, and Henry Ford.

These explorers and adventurers continue to push society and challenge mankind. I'm not saying that all innovation comes from these notable "superstar" thinkers, it also comes from the microcosm of boardrooms, research labs, and university programs where debate, diversity of opinion, disruptive thought, and discussion are creating new approaches to business. Think of Blue Nile with their crazy idea that people would buy $7,000 engagement rings online, without a sales associate, and have them delivered in the mail. Think of AmazonFresh offering to deliver groceries to your home in about an hour. Think how Apple, famous for bringing you the iPod and iPad, also summoned the power of the internet into the palm of your hand.

Think of car services like Uber and Lyft at your door in minutes because you summoned a driver to your exact location through an app on your phone. Consider Alexa—you can ask her to order Tide detergent for you or to tell you the annual rainfall in Nairobi, Kenya, or give you the meaning of the word *blatherskite*. Alexa is now your modern encyclopedia (for those of you saying, "Huh?" an encyclopedia was an entire series of books that was more or less very broad and shallow review of all knowledge-based data deemed highly sought after), dictionary, and internet errand girl all rolled into one. Tesla brought us high-end electric cars, and delivery drones (UAVs, unmanned aerial vehicles) have gone from prototype to planned investment as not-so-far-off solutions by Amazon, UPS, and even Domino's Pizza.[4]

These examples are no longer science fiction experiments, but now embedded into our lives, relied upon. In 1999 who would have thought people would trust the purchase of expensive jewelry online? Who would have imagined in 2007 that you could have computing power more sophisticated than an early (and cumbersome) desktop small enough to hold in the palm of your hand? In 2015, who envisioned ordering frozen foods and fresh, organic produce on the internet and having these things delivered to your door in half an hour? This takes imagination. To achieve these exploits requires passion, risk … and a healthy dose of diversity, discussion, and debate to go along with it. In a few short years, a delivery drone will take its place as a relic right alongside the Model T Ford. A flying car will be as ordinary to the consumer as purchasing a ticket on a passenger jet.

These kinds of advancements are possible only through the rich conversations of people who have different ideas and different experiences, different approaches to solving problems. If everyone thought alike, innovation could not happen. Imagine if every discussion was like that trip to Abilene, where no one spoke up to question why they were headed there to begin with. What if no one spoke up to offer a different view of the world or suggest the exploration of bold, new possibilities? It might look hauntingly similar to those hot, tired, frustrated folks stuffed in a car on a miserable drive from Dallas to Abilene, going where nobody wants to visit because no one spoke up and proposed a better alternative.

**IF EVERYONE THOUGHT ALIKE, INNOVATION COULD NOT HAPPEN**

# MINING DIVERSITY CREATES COLLABORATION

Think back, let's say after Adam and Eve, but before the invention of the wheel. Think cavemen. Imagine one of them squatting, rubbing sticks together, but those gathered around him squelched his pursuits. Seriously, think how foolish he must have looked for doing this. Imagine those looking on in wonder and amazement the first time someone ventured to test this concept? What would be the result had he given in to the pressure to stop trying? Imagine if Edison had yielded to peer pressure, or got too tired of finding all the ways his ideas didn't work to keep trying the next approach until one did? How about Steve Jobs?

Apple is world-renowned for their disruptive technology, founded by Jobs, one of the world's most innovative thinkers of all time. Apple's CEO, Tim Cook, knows that innovation begins with embracing—even celebrating—diversity. In his own words he describes it like this, "… if you're a CEO, the most important thing is to pick people around you that aren't like you, that complement you. Because you don't want to build a puzzle; you don't want to stack Chiclets up and have everyone be the same. And so I believe in diversity with a capital D."

Diversity of thought is stimulated by gathering people with a diversity of experiences; people from different races and cultures, different socioeconomic backgrounds and religious traditions, educational environments, and more. Add to that differences in learning style, communication style, temperament and personality. Bringing a group like that together takes one part courage and one part crazy, but if you can harness all that beautiful diversity through meaningful conversations and elevate the dialogue between them, you have an amazing opportunity before you. All that diversity is like a rich deposit of ore trapped in rock. Only by mining it can you be offered a spectrum of ideas to examine from which you can harvest true innovation.

I sit on the board of several organizations. Ten years ago, it was rare to find a woman on an executive board. Today, at least on boards where I am involved, at a minimum they seek to have at least thirty to forty percent of its members be female. Why? This isn't driven by equality in the workplace (though that is good thing), it is motivated by a more enlightened understanding that women have a deeper perspective of the female consumer. If you don't have enough female representation on the board, you lose the value of their viewpoint. Female board members walk, talk, and think differently than their male counterparts. They have a different approach to strategy, and their contributions elevate the awareness of male board members. Having them be part of the discussion makes the discussion better.

It doesn't stop there. Honoring diversity is not about satisfying a quota for gender or race, it is about understanding the value of bringing together people from many different backgrounds and experiences to improve the conversation and explore possibilities.

## GENERATIONAL DIVERSITY

There is much to be said about combining the stability that comes with experience with the originality and innovation that springs from youth. A fresh approach balanced with a seasoned method can yield great things.

I'll share later (see Teamwork) about when I went to Moosejaw and became their CEO. But in the discussion on diversity, it is relevant to note that when I went there I was forty-seven and the age of the average employee was about twenty-five years old. Coming in, I was the old guy. The company was floundering in the middle of the worst recession since the Great Depression, and my job was to engage with and support their culture to experience, have fun, and frolic while mentoring them and creating a stable platform from which they could continue working and enjoying their livelihood.

The generational diversity was a challenge at first, but as respect for what we each brought to the table grew, an understanding between us developed. As the leader, it was up to me to bridge that gap so they could trust me and allow me to harness all their fun, creative energy into a profitable endeavor without losing their culture.

To engage the team (and honestly to be me and live the life), I rode my bike to work from my hotel and back each day. The ride was twelve miles each way. For me biking is part of my life, for engaging the team, it was a clear signal I was young in heart (and conditioning). I may have been almost fifty, but I could in many cases "hang" with the young kids. Once at work I got out out of my lycra and clip in cycling shoes, showered, and went to work ... it was me and my authentic

**EMBRACING DIVERSITY DEMONSTRATES YOUR APPRECIATION FOR HOW OTHERS ENGAGE WITH THE WORLD**

life. About six months in we had a picnic in the back of the delivery dock. There was a keg involved, and plenty of beer. Now, keg-stands are not a normal practice for me, but in that context, I did one—and was the second longest keg-stand of the day. Whether it killed me or not, through these kinds of things I demonstrated to them that I appreciated how they engaged with the world.

I stretched myself to not just see things from their perspective, but also to experience them as they did. This gave me license to help them understand and respect the need to drive revenue, create profit, and pay attention to the bottom line. They could trust, listen to, and appreciate the relevance of me being there. I learned a great deal from them about cultivating a cult-like following and harnessing the viral-nature of social media as an integral part of a brand. These things proved valuable not only in the great turn-around for Moosejaw, but would serve me later when I would face the younger employee population as well as the younger age of Blue Nile's core customer.

# DEBATE YIELD DIVIDENDS

Embracing all of this diversity of opinion, debate, discussion, and dialogue is not to say, or even remotely suggest, that these conversations are easy. These conversations can be hard to navigate, but they are incredibly important. People own their ideas, and often feel protective of them. If you challenge an idea or don't adopt their idea, it can feel personal. This can threaten harmony in a team, so entertaining diverse perspectives can be tricky to navigate. But the best discoveries are often in the least-ventured waters.

Blue Nile had disrupted the jewelry industry. Founded on the concept that a customer would be willing to purchase an expensive ring online without physically touching it and trying it on had paid off. The company was a success. Because there were no brick-and-mortar store locations to buy or lease and maintain, no traditional sales force to employ, no meaningful inventory on the books, we required significantly lower working capital than our retail store counterparts. In a direct comparison to traditional jewelry stores, we had greatly reduced overhead and could pass that savings along to our customers and allow them to buy higher value items for fewer dollars. From the beginning, they never entertained the thought of any kind of brick-and-mortar experience.

For some customers, however, the inability to see the merchandise and try a ring on their finger was a deterrent to buying. Blue Nile's answer was to extend an already creative and disruptive element in the Blue Nile app called Dream Box. The app already had Dream Box which showed best selling rings to inspire consumers. When you shake your phone and are in the Dream Box, a new ring appears. On average the phone was shaken 26-27 times and the inspiration just grew and grew. The newest level of innovation to address the inability to see the merchandise and try a ring on their finger was embedded in the app and allowed a woman to take a picture of the Dream Box ring and see it on her finger. It

124

was cool. Every time the customer shook their phone now, the new ring which popped into the box could now be virtually "tried on" to their heart's content. Unfortunately, cool did not translate into conversion. Ultimately, the barrier of being unable to physically see, touch, and try on a ring was not answered through this technology.

So we strategized. Opinions were diverse, but further options sought by most to address the challenge were digitally oriented. One option proposed was testing something out in the brick and mortar retail environment. The board had never even thought of venturing into traditional retail, yet alone considered any thought of experimenting with a retail location. If we entered that territory and it was successful, then it could conceivably change the cost structure of the business, or so it was thought. It could fundamentally alter the cost of getting goods to market and therefore minimize the edge Blue Nile had of delivering such wonderful pricing to customers. Research pointed again and again to the thesis that the customers' inability to see, touch, and feel product directly impacted their trust to buy on-line and, in turn, from Blue Nile.

Through much conversation (and for sure some level of opposition), with a great deal of exploration and planning, through leveraging the diverse ideas, opinions, and experiences of the whole team, we eventually launched a plan in partnership with Nordstrom's flagship Seattle store to set up a small display (6 ft. x 2 ft.) to test a stop-in-and-shop concept. The investment was relatively small with low risk, and greatly minimized the add-on variables of lease/rent costs and traditional sales compensation structure, and so we proceeded. Even though we didn't have total consensus from everyone that this was a good idea or that the idea would even work, the team trusted each other and believed this was an option worth exploring.

The Blue Nile culture allowed room for the talent and innovation of diverse team members to play out. One of the lead directors confided to me two years after that initial experiment that he didn't really understand it at the time and wasn't really on board with it. However, because he believed I was doing an effective job at leading, because he saw the risk was relatively low, and because we hadn't yet uncovered a path to answer the customer's challenge to trust buying on-line more, it seemed appropriate to proceed. Even though he didn't really believe the plan would work at the time, he was willing to venture the experiment, trusting the value of the team. This is the fruitfulness of diversity and debate in action (and in my book, the mark of a great board member and partner)!

I am happy to report that the experiment was a success and we followed up with another pop-up in a New York Nordstrom's. With the success of these shop-in-shop concepts, we moved farther forward in our exploration and tested the concept even deeper by opening Blue Nile's first free-standing showroom concept. Today there are six of them, and they are very different from the size and set-up of traditional jewelry stores. The evolution of the showrooms continues to evolve with new thinking, new debate. The culture of Blue Nile which opens its arms to diversity and debate has allowed them to embrace forward-thinking concepts and remain on the cutting edge of the retail brand. The showrooms fit into a larger strategic plan to address see, touch, and feel and likely will continue to evolve and transition. The success of Blue Nile is grounded in their continual evolution with new thinking, debate based in real and open conversation, and dialogue. These are of great benefit.

## ALLOWING DIVERSITY CULTIVATES OPPORTUNITY

Leading people in sharing their views, risking that they may be misunderstood or that their view may not be appreciated by others, is a critical leadership skill. The collaborative process does not just happen. It must be nurtured. Leaders must guide debate, discussion, and dialogue about what is important, how to achieve goals—when, at what cost, and through what means. The leader's role is to host the debate, engaging all at the table to share and to listen, to contribute and to absorb. Sometimes these conversations are direct and straightforward. Sometimes they are more nuanced and may require several rounds of discourse. Some people venture this territory willingly, while others must be encouraged along. There will always be some contingent who struggles and comes along begrudgingly, if at all. Whatever the case, encouraging these kinds of conversations and holding them as valuable will allow a culture of diversity to evolve. As the community takes shape, members of the team will begin to appreciate the value of diversity of thought and opinion.

Celebrating diversity and stimulating collaboration requires that defensive barriers be lowered. In this, you must lead by example. Self-preservation raises walls. If people are content to stay with what is comfortable, when they know what feels safe, they cannot explore the treasures of thought undiscovered, the wealth of ideas untapped. As in all things leadership related, being comfortable with being uncomfortable is an asset.

In encouraging diversity and fostering dialogue a leader guides and counsels. By honoring different points of view a leader instills confidence and enthusiasm. This thriving culture of diversity helps create momentum and inspires others to be the best they can be. A leader who learns to encourage diversity of thought, create discourse, and celebrate different points of view invites unlimited possibilities to explore and opens wide the gates of innovation.

Innovation brings me back to the subject of adventure and the critical (and often overlooked) role it plays in the quality of a leader. Without realizing it, my orientation toward adventure from a young age has become foundational to my approach to leadership. In the next chapter,

I'll tell you about the time I climbed Mt. Rainier and how racing cars is a lot like running a company. In the process, I hope to whet your appetite for adventure and challenge you to engage in experiences that will further develop your curiosity and test both your agility and resilience—all of which will cause you to grow as a leader.

## ENDNOTES

1. *50 Years of the Jetsons: Why The Show Still Matters* by Matt Novak. © 2012 Smithsonian.com. https://www.smithsonianmag.com/history/50-years-of-the-jetsons-why-the-show-still-matters-43459669/. Posted on 09/19/12. Retrieved from the web 09/22/18.

2. Ibid.

3. Ibid.

4. *Amazon and UPS are Betting Big on Drone Delivery* by Jeff Desjardins, Visual Capitalist. © 2018 Business Insider. https://www.businessinsider.com/amazon-and-ups-are-betting-big-on-drone-delivery-2018-3. Posted 03/11/18. Retrieved from the web 09/25/18.

# Chapter Twelve

# ADVENTURE
## CREATING THE AGILITY TO BECOMING A CATALYST FOR CHANGE

"I have discovered that even the mediocre can
have adventures and even the fearful can achieve.
You don't have to be a hero to accomplish
great things—to compete. You can
just be an ordinary chap, sufficiently
motivated to reach challenging goals."

**SIR EDMUND HILLARY**
Mountaineer, Explorer, Philanthropist

Trying things new and unfamiliar stimulates subconscious problem-solving, forcing you to see things from a new point of view. Adventure develops your curiosity and tests both your agility and resilience. Adventure builds confidence, not so much by having one big grand adventurous experience, but by engagement in many, many smaller adventures which prove invaluable in your family, your work and life. The cumulative value of these experiences is driven by what you do, where you do it, who you do it with, when you do it, ... you get the point; but as you have these "adventures" you gain perspective, and hopefully with this, develop intuition.

Intuition is grasping a situation immediately and reaching a conclusion without a conscious reasoning process. Some of this happens through instinct, but it also comes from the summation of your life's experiences and how you have processed those experiences. This creates a context which allows you to sense (intuit) the next move. It's your gut feeling—a hunch. Some discredit intuition as part of decision-making, concerned that feelings or emotions could cause you to make a potentially misguided choice. However, if intuition is formed through the sum total of your life's experiences, then that "gut feeling" is really your body of knowledge, an instantly accessed cellular encyclopedia of all the facts you know and how applying them turned out in the past. In this light, intuition is a powerful beacon, not just a nudge in the direction of where you think the wind is blowing.

Intuition is not the same thing as insight per se', because insight is linked to a deep understanding of things, beyond taking in data or quick observation. Insight is developed in the context of how events happened, what knowledge was gained from those, then recombining this knowledge in different ways. You start with your gut-feeling, your intuition, then call upon your insight to look at things from a different angle and see what applies. Your intuition summed up the situation, telling you what problem needed to be solved. Your insight creates an event-driven, "A-ha!" moment outcome which allows you to solve the problem your intuition defined.

While both intuition and insight are driven by your experiences, they help you in slightly different ways. In combination, they provide "your gut"—your intellect and base of knowledge to look at things differently and apply what is relevant to any given situation. How you use your intuition drives how you process data and leads to those "Eureka!" moments which provide keen insight to create out-of-the-box outcomes.

**ADVENTURE IMPRINTS YOUR MIND IN POWERFUL WAYS, CREATING KEY REFERENCE POINTS AND GIVING YOU A BOLD SPIRIT**

Every experience you have becomes part of your intuition and insight, but experiences that live up to the word "adventure" indicates something greater. Adventure is something more exciting, potentially unusual, and therefore stands out and makes a deep impression on you, creates your "gut," something you can trust. Steve Jobs said, "You have to trust in something—your gut, destiny, life and karma, whatever. This approach has never let me down, and it has made all the difference in my life." Adventure is a riskier undertaking with more uncertain outcomes. These experiences imprint your mind in powerful ways, creating a richer context than the more predictable experiences encountered daily on the meandering road of life. Adventure creates key reference points and gives you a bold spirit.

## SPIRIT, SPUNK, AND A SUMMIT VICTORY

I climbed Mt. Rainier when I was sixteen. The National Park Services states that about 10,000 people attempt the summit each year with only about half succeeding. Every season several people die along the various routes up the mountain.[1] My parents signed me up for an eight-week, cross-country, outward-bound kind of trip. There were seven in my group along with a leader/counselor who was just a few years older than we were. We were on week six of the adventure together, teenagers all, and in pretty good shape.

We hiked up to a spot about 10,000 feet up where we took shelter at Camp Muir, a well-known base camp for those attempting to reach the mountain's summit. We arrived around 4:30 in the afternoon, had dinner, and by 7:00 PM, it was lights out. The altitude and vigorous exercise made us glad to crawl into our sleeping bags and close our eyes. It seemed like only minutes had passed when they woke us up at midnight to start the final ascent. We got into our gear with headlamps attached to our helmets so we could see in the dark, crampons fastened to our boots, and ice axes in hand to help us have enough traction to hike up the glacier. It was difficult and dangerous … and exhilarating! In spite of the seven of us having made Camp Muir, along the climb on day two, three decided they could not handle the intensity and make the full climb. They turned around mid-way on the second day—and midway of the "second day" was around 3:00 a.m. Don't forget the beginning of day two was really the middle of the night, a big test of endurance!

As the rest of us soldiered on, we were split into two groups with the guides and all of us were roped up together within our groups. I was making progress on a pretty steep section of the mountain when I mis-stepped and fell back. I slid on my ass for what seemed a good number of feet before I self-arrested—turned over on my front and dug my ice axe into the glacier. I stopped. Panting. My heart raced from the exercise, the altitude, and the adrenalin. It had all happened in a few seconds, but the memory of those seconds are as fresh in my mind now as they were when I was fifteen. That was a scary moment, but the potential of sliding how far to who-knows-what end was not enough to make me want to quit or turn back. We took a break for a rest around 3:00 a.m. (when half the team turned back). We rested for just two short hours before making the final leg of the climb to the top of the mountain. I was there to reach the summit and exhilarated to stand at the top. We made it!

The thrill of reaching for a goal has always pushed me to push past the risks of the journey to reach it.

# A SERIES OF INCREDIBLE ADVENTURES

Adventure was part of my family's core fabric. It wasn't just outdoor excursions that fed this, but the willingness to embrace totally new (and inconvenient) things to succeed. My dad's drive for accomplishment and success led our family to make more than one significant geographical relocation. The first I remember was when I was about nine or ten when dad relocated us from the metropolis of New York on Long Island to a town with a population of about 100,000 people out in the middle of nowhere. We packed up and moved to Allouez, Wisconsin, a suburb of Green Bay, and settled in a small Jewish community there. A great big adventure for my family, to say the least!

Here we encountered people who were considered the salt of the earth. It was the land of Vince Lombardi and the Green Bay Packers—even though my mom was a devout Giants fan—I can still remember her yelling at the top of her lungs while we watched games. Allouez was a dairy town, full of farmers and much different than the people who made up the Long Island community where I grew up. There my parents built a wonderful house.

My dad was an apparel merchant and traveled extensively, often outside the States to Europe. Late one night while he was away, I was awakened from a sound sleep to my mother squealing my name, "Haaaaa-rr-veeeyyy!!" Being from the city, she had not had much occasion for encounters with mice inside the house. Well, our new home was right across the street from a big farm surrounded by barbed wire. Our cats had ventured into their barn and proudly returned bringing home two mice with which to surprise my mother. To this day I can remember her running around in her nightie, my sister and I chasing the mice trying desperately to catch them.

In fact, my early years were full of adventure, and the move to Green Bay was not to be our last. About five years in we moved again. This time we went to Minneapolis so my dad could take advantage of new career opportunities. Along the way I did everything from car camping at Mt. Rushmore in the Badlands as a family to rock climbing in the Tetons with my other outdoor adventure group. I remember our family taking trips to International Falls, Minnesota (bordering Canada) to fish for Walleye and Muskie. We would fillet the fish right there, lakeside, and cook it up fresh for lunch. When it came time to consider colleges, my mom and I took a road trip across country to visit campuses. All these adventures together created a high level of change agility in me which has served me well throughout life.

The concept of adventure has progressed throughout my life as I have given myself from one immersive experience to the next. I ran my own business detailing cars and by the time I was eighteen, I had bought and sold twenty-one cars. A few weeks into college I found a girlfriend and two weeks after graduation, made her my wife. During college I had an internship working for Target Stores which helped set up my early career in retail where I spent eight years with Carter Hawley Hale (in eight different roles). I went on to work for two years with Sears in their pursuit to become a national department store. From there I enjoyed eight years with Eddie Bauer where I had the wonderful experience to be part of Seattle University's Center for Leadership Graduate Program. That led to the opportunity to serve as President of Aaron Brothers Art & Framing for three years, followed by three more years with the world's largest craft retailer, Michaels (and a battle with cancer). After that I joined the team as CEO of Moosejaw, then went on to Blue Nile. Each of these roles in every company required a move to a new city, a new adventure, and embracing new life experiences.

During these career adventures and moves, my wife and I had three children, two bar mitzvahs and one bat mitzvah, confirmations, school events, and everything else that goes along with raising a family. I pursued my passion for cars, motorcycles, and motorsports which gave entrance to racing Formula Fords; first on my own, then with my family track-

side with me each weekend. My son, Zak, raced go-karts, then as he got older started racing with me. In the beginning, he was usually in my rear view mirror, but as time went by, he oh-so-quickly ran out in front of me as the young gun mastered his craft.

I ran marathons, ventured a 100-mile bike ride to test myself—my fortitude and resolve—while raising money to help find a cure for the

disease that had threatened to take my life. And lately, 3 mile runs with my youngest daughter, Maddie, have turned into 7-8 mile hikes in the Cascades, never a dull moment.

Through all these things, I have learned to look at life as a series of adventures. Each day holds incredible new possibilities. I relish the opportunity to embrace diversity, to see things from a different perspective, and boldly accept new experiences as an exciting part of the rhythm of life. It has never occurred to me to be any other way.

# RACING CARS AND RUNNING COMPANIES

One of my preferred adventures surrounds my passion for racing cars, with one of my favorite quotes being by Mario Andretti. He said, "If everything seems under control, you're just not going fast enough." I find this to be true whether racing along a predefined track in a car or following a retail plan in business; you are moving on a course at an accelerated clip where unexpected things come up rapidly and force you to react or crash.

In amateur racing, drivers get two practice runs, then we run the course once more to qualify for the starting position, then we race. In my race car, I could be coming down the track at 130 m.p.h. and as I approach a turn, I might see two cars crash right in front of me. I have to react to avoid or collide. Sometimes the car doesn't work as anticipated, it may handle differently than it did during practice. I might lose a gear or my tires might wear out. I must navigate the context of the situation at hand. The races I drive in are forty-five miles long and last about thirty minutes. Any longer than that would require a pit stop, which means employing a pit crew and mechanics which becomes very expensive. So, whatever situation comes up while driving, I must  make constant adjustments in order to finish. On a course with no pit stops, if you pull over, you lose the race.

This is not unlike retail on any given day. Things transpire that do not go according to plan. You might start a promotion in the morning, but the event is so successful the traffic takes the website down or you run out of goods. A delivery may arrive later than planned, or the quality of a shipment may be bad. Whatever comes up, you are required to make constant adjustments within the context of a larger plan. You can't pull over or you'll lose. Just as a sailboat must constantly tack, zig-zagging across the water to catch the wind, in business you must make constant continuous corrections to handle the unexpected to keep your momentum. The way you envision it going and the way it actually happens are not often the same. Just as in racing, execution is the difference between being great and being good.

So, if everything in your business is completely under control, then you are not moving fast enough. If you can anticipate every obstacle and navigate smoothly through every twist and turn, then you are not taking enough risks. In fact, in racing, perhaps a little technical, but the reality is that the coefficient of adhesion is such that the fastest way around a track is not just on the edge, but constantly just barely sliding…not sliding much, but just enough that the car is almost gliding over the asphalt. The reality is that tires and asphalt work by creating a coefficient of grip, adhesion … too much adhesion slows the car down, too little and the car slides off the track, but just the right slip angle and *voila*, you may qualify on the pole and win the race. It most certainly is a fine line between being "on the edge, and over the edge", but that's racing.

Adventure creates an orientation towards risk, that isn't the same thing as chance. While there is inherent risk in racing cars, taking risks is not the same as leaving things to chance. Preparation takes the chance out of risk. Before racing for thirty minutes, I will have spent eight to ten hours testing and making adjustments, preparing for an event. Embracing risk acknowledges that if I don't race I can't win. The risk is that even if I have perfectly prepared the car, bought new tires, and had textbook practice runs, there is still the possibility of something going wrong. I have had crashes, some bad ones. Thankfully, I have not sustained injury though others involved did. I embrace the risk and love the inherent requirement of speed, danger, and desire to win, putting every ounce of this energy into focus until it is second nature to choose the right line and successfully drive the turn.

The preparation to race is not unlike the preparation that goes into getting ready for Black Friday, Cyber Monday, or other major retail events like Valentine's or Mother's Day. There

**VERY LITTLE SEPARATES THE BIG WINNERS FROM THE BOTTOM OF THE PACK**

is an almost extreme level of planning and coordinating to successfully execute one of these events. You prepare for months for a single day of sales. Everyone else in retail is doing the same thing, all in the same race with you. You have to capture attention and translate that into sales and the stakes are high. As in racing, very little separates the big winners from the bottom of the pack. If things go well, these events set up a stretch of positive earnings. Gone bad they could cause you to spiral for the next season. The win is worth the risk.

Jeff Bezos, CEO of Amazon said, "I knew that if I failed I wouldn't regret that, but I knew the one thing I might regret is not trying." Your tolerance for risk is directly related to your ability to be successful. In fact, not taking risks may be the riskiest thing you could do in business. Having a bent toward adventure gives you an orientation toward taking risks.

## CONNECTING THE DOTS

When you go into something with an unknown quality, relish that adventure and learn from it. Life's experiences create wisdom, expand knowledge, and broaden perspective. The rich, deep diversity in you resulting from having an adventurous spirit allows you to be a catalyst for change when you find yourself in a position where something is not working. Adventure requires you to respond, to think about what you need to do, and how to react. It forces you to think at a deeper, more profound level and gives you an appreciation of context. In an unknown environment, your comfort level is pushed and good leaders are okay with that.

To lead people effectively, you have to use all the means at your disposal to successfully navigate a path from here to there. Adventure informs your intuition and insight and creates an agility in you. You must become comfortable being uncomfortable. "If you want to be a powerful leader, you have to become familiar with the sweat-inducing, anxiety-producing, adrenalin-generating emotions of being lost while people are following you."[2] Leaders love an adventure.

There is no doubt in my mind that the adventurous soul is predisposed to action. The agility gained through navigating adventure creates the confidence needed to act, even when there is a high degree of uncertainty, a significant element of risk, or the need to respond before all the facts can be gathered and weighed. Adventure wires you to act. You can never reach high-levels of leadership without the consistent ability to take action.

In the next chapter, I'll tell a story about a pilot who had only seconds to act and hanging in the balance were the lives of 155 people. We'll discuss how a leader influences a culture of action and can create a safe place for team members to embrace the outcomes of their actions, succeed or fail. Fostering a spirit of adventure is crucial for encouraging this important quality of action.

## ENDNOTES

1. *About Mt. Rainier.* Mt. Rainier FAQ, Washington State, US, 14,411 feet. © 1999-2018 Alan Arnette. http://www.alanarnette.com/climbs/rainierfaq.php Retrieved from the web 09/20/18.

2. *The Emotional Adventure of Leadership.* Peter Bregman. Harvard Business Law Review, June 14, 2012. https://hbr.org/2012/06/the-emotional-adventure-of-lea.html?awid=5286744549534879728-3271. Retrieved from the web 09/18/18.

# Chapter Thirteen

# DECISIVENESS
## TAKING ACTION AND ACCOUNTABILITY

"Every morning in Africa, a gazelle wakes up,
it knows it must outrun the fastest lion or it
will be killed. Every morning in Africa, a lion
wakes up. It knows it must run faster than the
slowest gazelle, or it will starve. It doesn't matter
whether you're the lion or a gazelle—when the
sun comes up, you'd better be running."

**CHRISTOPHER MCDOUGALL**
Journalist and Author of Born to Run: A Hidden Tribe, Superathletes,
and the Greatest Race the World Has Never Seen

Actions are the truest reflection of values—where communication is proved. What you do as a leader is every bit as important as what you say. You lead by example. An action-oriented leader creates an action-oriented team. Decisiveness in a leader is a requirement for sustaining successful outcomes. Leaders must make challenging decisions, sometimes in less-than-ideal circumstances and faced with unknown factors. Leaders must balance emotion and reason and be able to act quickly with available information while relying on their intuition and experience to make good decisions in difficult situations.

How a leader acts and reacts sets the tone for the entire organization. A leader's mood is contagious and resonates with those around, establishing the emotional climate. Leaders are not immune to feelings of anxiety and they possess a keen awareness of the downside, but strong leaders learn to manage their emotional state so feelings don't muddy the waters when they need to think clearly and act decisively.

Long-range, strategic planning allows for a thoughtful, measured, explore-all-the-options process in decision making. A leader must have the big picture in mind, be fully versed in and committed to the execution of this long-term strategy while willing to make quick decisions that come up at the lightning pace of business. Acting and reacting often requires a quick assessment of context to respond to real-life, real-time scenarios without the luxury of deliberation. These decisions drive the resulting level of action down through the layers of the organization. Conversely, when a leader falters when making or communicating decisions, this trickles down through the ranks as uncertainty and results in a paralysis of action.

## WIRED TO ACT

Have you ever worked in an environment where people do not act, instead waiting to be told to do so? What motivates you to action? How do you function when you are in an environment where the work is largely undefined? Do you set the pace for yourself or do others set it for you? Can you juggle variables easily or does uncertainty throw you off balance? Is there a fire in your belly?

The answers to this stream of questions reveals whether or not a person is wired to act or wired to wait. While everyone can develop skills, increase their EQ, and grow as a leader, not everyone is wired to lead at high levels. There is an element of nature (not just nurture) at play in whether or not a person has the natural orientation to make decisions and take action. Many people are not great at making decisions. High-level leadership operates in a high-risk environment that puts a leader into vulnerable positions, their actions are on display and the results of their decisions have high stakes. Not everyone is cut out for this. Not everyone is willing to take the risk of failure and accept the requirements to communicate the vision, the plan, and the measurement of results against goals. Many people do not desire the responsibilities that come with being in a senior role.

As you go upward, more is required from you. It's true that great rewards often come as the result of high-risk endeavors. But a desire for great reward does not necessarily ensure one has the fortitude, perseverance, and skills required to embrace the elements of navigating high risk. High stakes are not for the faint of heart. Consequences for those in high-level leadership are broad and visible. Leaders do not take action simply for the possible reward, leaders act because they are in a position requiring them to lead and they cannot help but answer the call.

## EIGHT SECONDS

John Maxwell said, "A leader is one who knows the way, goes the way, and shows the way." A mark of a great leader is the confidence to make a decision, act, and embrace accountability for those decisions and actions. In 2009, US Airways flight 1549 took off from New York's LaGuardia airport on a cold January day and encountered a flock of geese which took out the engines. The pilot, Sully Sullenberger, made the decision to land on the Hudson River. All 155 people on board survived the crash landing into the frigid water[1] (the temperature in New York that day was only about twenty degrees).

His initial contact with air traffic control after the bird strike was a mayday announcing the need to turn back to LaGuardia, and he was given clearance to do so. Less than a minute and half passed before he informed control they couldn't make it back and inquired about heading "toward New Jersey maybe Teterboro?" because it was closer. The official transcript of Flight 1549 cockpit communications shows a brief eight seconds between Sully's affirmative response to head for Teterboro and his next words delivered over the plane's public address system, "This is the Captain, brace for impact."[2] Eight seconds.

Most of us need more time than that to decide what we want for lunch. Making the decision to crash land a plane in the Hudson River with the lives of 154 people in your charge under that kind of pressure is an extraordinary circumstance. In this day of modern technology, carefully guided systems with every-case-scenario procedures, we tend to think planes practically fly themselves. Yet in this instance, the fate of all passengers and crew (and potentially others who may be in the crash path) was in the hands of one leader—the captain. He had no time for second-guessing, no time for deliberation and debate, he had to make a series of decisions from the depth of his experience and intuition. Inaction would mean death for all on board. He had to act.

The entire scenario from the first bird strike to the initial impact of a water landing took just under three and a half minutes to play out. Relying on their training to save everyone on board, the response of Captain Sully and his crew was to act decisively. In a much later interview Sullenberger said, "... he worked sometimes wordlessly with his first officer, Jeff Skiles, in dividing urgent chores despite never having flown together before ... 'We were able to collaborate wordlessly,' Sullenberger said, 'I didn't have time to direct his every action ... You have to deal with the most time-critical things first ... Situational awareness is the ability to see the entirety of the forest, but knowing at any given moment which tree is the most important one.'"[3] Then, in the historic tradition of captains, Sully did not abandon ship—leave the plane—until he was sure everyone on board had first been safely evacuated.[4]

Sully was a hero. He wasn't trying to be a hero, he was just being a leader and his leadership was heroic. In the aftermath, his decisions were picked apart. He was under the scrutiny of an entire nation while authorities challenged his decision not to return to the airport, but land on the water. He had seconds to make decisions—not minutes, not hours, not days. He had to act, and he was accountable for every life on board that plane as well as for following protocols and being responsible for the aircraft itself. There is a heavy mantle of responsibility that goes with leadership.

## FOSTERING ACTION

Through each of our discussions about leadership characteristics, there is always a connection back to the culture a leader creates. A culture that is built around trust, learning, empathy, and empowerment must equally be built around the willingness to act and live with the outcomes—succeed or fail. When leaders decide, act, and set a course, things do not always work out as expected. Leaders who own their decisions and are accountable for their actions demonstrate humility through their vulnerability. When you are sure of the destination, those who follow trust you to steer the ship, even when that means making a mid-term course correction during navigation. This transparency creates an environment that encourages people to take risks, deal with mistakes,

> A CULTURE BUILT AROUND TRUST, LEARNING, EMPATHY, AND EMPOWERMENT MUST ALSO HAVE THE WILL TO ACT AND LIVE WITH THE OUTCOMES—SUCCEED OR FAIL

and learn without fear of retribution or punishment. An orientation for action is championed.

In that culture, people will learn. They will make mistakes and accept accountability and through that, grow and develop into the kind of leaders you want and need. This is a healthy environment where who you work with and where you work is inspiring. The long-term viability of a business or organization with this positive, action-rewarding culture is much more sound.

In much the same way that Captain Sully's crew took their cues from him, his co-pilot responding even without words exchanging between them, a leader's actions communicate priorities to their team. John Quincy Adams said, "If your actions inspire others to dream more, learn more, do more, and become more, you are a leader." When a leader acts—does something that needs doing—they establish a precedent to take action and not wait for someone else to act first. Their leadership is supported and defined by action, not just words. By their actions, good leaders challenge people to push beyond their own borders.

## THE BUCK STOPS HERE

President Harry S. Truman had a sign on his desk that read: "The Buck Stops Here." He was of that rare breed of leader who accepted responsibility for every decision and action made by those in his administration. Accountability is the obligation of an individual or organization to account for its activities, accept responsibility for them, and to disclose the results transparently. It also includes the responsibility for money or other entrusted property.[5] In short, it means a leader embraces responsibility for all the outcomes of their choices. These kind of leaders question all decisions and processes which shape an organization, seeking success for the whole, not looking to cast blame or call negative attention to mistakes. Instead they address things. They fix things. Like Truman, they accept responsibility for the performance of the organization, goals met or missed.

Accountability requires vulnerability. Self-awareness and honest review of both successes and failures allow leaders to resolve conflicts, meet challenges, and create solutions to problems. Communication is vital to transparency. Frequent communication is needed—thoughtful, relevant, authentic communication. There must be a plan in place, a plan that is mutually agreed upon and understood. Accountability requires that goals set are communicated clearly. What are the milestones along the way? What are the metrics by which we measure progress? What happens if we meet goals? Miss them?

Accountable leaders must have the ability to create dialogue with members of their team. When outcomes are reached you communicate, "Way to go! Well done … This happened faster/better than I anticipated!" It also means you address and modify expectations when things are off-track or not working. You have conversations, sometimes hard ones, with those who are consistently missing the mark. "Listen, you are a wonderful person, but there seems to be a lack of commitment here …" Whether there is an element missing regarding their work ethic, or a lack of will or skill, members of a team must each be held accountable for their outcomes. If this person remains in their position, the whole team suffers. If a leader leaves someone in place who is a drag on the team, morale falls, productivity drops, and respect for that leader comes into question.

Accountability fosters perpetual refinement and delivers on a commitment to excellence. Decision making. Action. Accountability. These three elements are hand-in-hand requirements for all good leaders. Accountability builds trust. Accountability for actions creates respect between leaders and their teams, and teamwork is the whole point of leadership to begin with.

In the next chapter, I'll share the Moosejaw story I promised you in the chapter on diversity. Through it I'll illustrate the value of teamwork and show you how to get the best out of the people for which you are accountable to lead. It is vital to understand that each team member is a valued contributor, an important ingredient in the recipe. A leader who is free from self-interest and not full of ego can pull people together into a cohesive team and together, achieve great things. Ultimately, your desire to be part of something greater is contagious, and others are inspired to be part of that team.

## ENDNOTES

1. *The Miracle on the Hudson. 2009: Airplane crash-lands into Hudson River; all aboard reported safe.* Published January 15, 2009. CNN. https://www.cnn.com/2016/08/11/us/hudson-landing-archive-news-story/index.html. Retrieved from the web 09/14/18.

2. *Excerpts of Flight 1549 Cockpit Communications.* Posted 06/09/2009 by The Associated Press. http://usatoday30.usatoday.com/news/nation/2009-06-09-hudson-cockpit-transcript_N.htm. Retrieved from the web 09/14/18.

3. *Miracle on the Hudson pilot Sully Sullenberger: Southwest crew worked seamlessly to land jet.* Bart Jansen, USA Today. Published 4:24 PM ET April 19, 2018. https://www.usatoday.com/story/news/2018/04/19/sully-sullenberger-southwest-airlines-emergency-landing/533821002/. Retrieved from the web 09/14/18.

4. *The Miracle on the Hudson. 2009: Airplane crash-lands into Hudson River; all aboard reported safe.* Published January 15, 2009. CNN. https://www.cnn.com/2016/08/11/us/hudson-landing-archive-news-story/index.html. Retrieved from the web 09/14/18.

5. Accountability. http://www.businessdictionary.com/definition/accountability.html. Retrieved from the web 09/16/18.

Chapter Fourteen

# TEAMWORK
## IT'S ALL ABOUT US, WE, AND *ESPRIT DE CORPS*

"Teamwork is the ability to work together
toward a common vision. The ability to direct
individual accomplishments toward organizational
objectives. It is the fuel that allows common
people to attain uncommon results."

**ANDREW CARNEGIE**
Industrialist, Business Magnate, Philanthropist

The French call it *esprit de corps*. In a team there is enthusiasm around common interests and responsibilities. There is a feeling of pride, fellowship, and common loyalty that is shared by members of a team. Put simply, we are better together. Brainstorming allows people to access new ideas that would likely remain dormant and unexplored if not stimulated by group collaboration. Sharing discoveries and meeting goals together is more fun. In a team you belong to something greater than yourself. The energy and camaraderie of a team helps people push past individual limitations they might not venture beyond if left on their own. Because the strengths of everyone on the team are at the disposal of the team, productivity can thrive. Teamwork harnesses the power of multiplication and creates leverage. While the ultimate leader cannot in reality share the risk, the risk-taking can be minimized when the team's insight, perspective, and knowledge are leveraged. Because team members are not sticking their necks out alone, individuals often feel braver and more courageous under this umbrella. Let's consider this concept.

# A LONE BABOON IS A DEAD BABOON

Alone, a single baboon is easy prey for a lion, leopard, or cheetah. In a troop, that baboon is safe. Within that troop, one baboon is recognized to lead the efforts to protect; you might even say the leader guides and counsels, instills confidence and enthusiasm in troop members. Stay with me now …

Baboons are social creatures. You simply do not find a baboon taking up residence all alone out in the wilderness. They live in troops with a clear leader and an organizational social hierarchy. Baboons communicate with each other constantly, with scientists observing more than thirty distinct vocalizations in addition to numerous recognizable non-vocal gestures.[1] Their troops form cohesive units that move together in columns of two or three, fanning out as they search for food.[2] This social structure has several functions, but of chief importance is protection from predators. Living in a troop significantly decreases the risk of becoming prey. The troop has more individuals on the lookout for predators, so they are detected more quickly. Lookouts sound the alarm and the troop either runs together for safety, or collectively rally to face the predator as a mob and drive it away.[3]

I know of no CEO who describes his team as "baboon-like" on the company website, but leadership is present in Baboon Troops for certain. Let's pull apart the leadership lessons demonstrated above by the troop and their "top baboon" and examine a fresh "baboon leadership" perspective. Consider these elements:

| BABOON TROOP | SUCCESSFUL BUSINESS COHORT |
|---|---|
| Baboons are highly agile. | Team members are highly agile (flexible). |
| Baboons can run at high speeds. | Team members can navigate the fast pace of business. They can run faster and better together to achieve more. |
| To stay alive, Baboon Troops are constantly vigilant, keeping an eye out for predators (lions, leopards, cheetahs, etc.) | To stay alive (compete), members are constantly vigilant, keeping an eye out for predators (competitors, outdated systems, unimaginative marketing, etc.) |
| Baboon Troop members each have a defined role (lookouts, foragers, groomers, etc.) | Each team members has a defined role. Roles stratify vertically and spread out horizontally to create reporting relationships and functional organization; but regardless, each role defined individually ultimately sums to a team, team members aggregate as a unit. |
| Baboons communicate clearly with each other. | Team members communicate clearly with each other. |
| Baboon Troops ban together around a rallying cry to fight as a pack, fiercely defend their troop, and meet their goals of survival and success (defend against attacking predators). | Teams band together around a rallying cry, a vision unifies them as one, and together they meet their defined goals for survival and success (profitability, performance, etc.). |

While a baboon troop is certainly not a mirror-image of corporate life, to fiercely defend, be agile, run fast, compete, be on the lookout, and sound an alarm are in many ways, attributes of a leader and a unified team. Regardless of whether or not you buy this loose analogy, one thing is clear—a lone baboon is a dead baboon. A self-interested, dictatorial, smarter-than-everyone-else-in-the-room, un-engaged, non-empathetic, unaware "baboon" is a leader with a short future. In today's business climate, those following a more progressive leadership model are the leaders who will rise to the top.

## THERE REALLY IS NO "I" IN TEAM

From the beginning, I have defined leadership as setting a course for others to follow. Leaders help to define what can be done together as a team. Collaborative leadership encourages members to contribute ideas and strategy, ultimately crafting the path others will follow to reach a common goal or destination. There is a big picture and it has many moving parts. All those moving parts must understand how they fit into the big picture. The big picture is only clear when all the parts are in the right places.

Leaders communicate the big picture, set the course, and then facilitate following this course by offering support for what it is going to look like and how the team is going to get there. Within a team, the leader serves to guide and counsel, to instill confidence and enthusiasm, to create momentum and inspiration for others in their desire to be the best they can be. In short, they empower people to work together to accelerate the crafting, development, and execution of a strategy.

Notice I did not say that the leader has to be "the one" (the "I") who singularly defines the what, how, and when. The leader does not just tell others what to do, they are not separate from the team. The leader is part of the team—one ingredient in the recipe for creating the outcome (common goal or destination). All parts of the recipe are dependent on "the team" as a whole. A good leader facilities the talents and abilities of each member of their team, allowing them to contribute to the course they follow. A strong leader supports the what, how, and when in regards to the vision, but they have no need to be the all-knowing, smartest-person-in-the-room who has to have all the answers.

While at Moosejaw, it was my objective to turn the company around and make it profitable without destroying their unique culture. Without changing the recipe of their "secret sauce" that had generated a cult-like following in their customers, I needed to lead the development of a new revised proforma, crunch the numbers, address gross margins, and make the business work. I needed to understand and leverage the culture, respecting it for all the power it had while figuring out how to run the company differently. It would have been impossible to achieve this on my own, or by simply handing down directives and asking people to toe the line. Only by leveraging the talents and perspectives of the existing team could we hope to bring structure and thoughtful planning to bear without screwing up the culture. If you have not been on the Moosejaw site you should check it out. The online experience was and remains quirky and humorous; it is an incredibly engaging experiential interaction. From Facebook, to Instragam, and really across all social media interaction, the brand has created a community excited about being identified with Moosejaw.

As the leader, it was my job to direct the evolution to the vision for what could drive a plan, process and discipline to return sales growth and profit across the on-line and brick-and-mortar channels. While the task at hand was "the business" and returning sales and profit, over time, with success we began to undertake even greater explorations to achieve greater growth and higher profits. As a retailer, Moosejaw led the digital wave "with mobile first" as the priority. We as a team, and leveraging the culture of innovation, disruption, and creativity created an agile "technical philosophy." We created a responsive digital platform and even executed the first 3-D catalog with a unique consumer experience using the iphone's interface. In the brick and mortar channel, we envisioned a different type of store, a different type of experience. I led the charge to discover how we could create a three-dimensional version of that online experience in a store environment, but the team led the development of bringing Moosejaw's cult-like following along into the new store prototype. I led the team, challenging them to find ways we could maintain that kind of exceptional engagement and enthusiastic interaction with customers in a live retail experience, but recognized the incredible leverage they brought to the party in accomplishing this work.

We created a cohort of people, made up from a cross-section of the company: from executives and junior management as well as from those who worked in the customer call center and warehouse. Humor was a huge part of the Moosejaw experience. When you called in (and to this day) you are greeted with an unexpected "Mooooooose-Jaw" as a hello. If you get put on hold, instead of elevator music, you hear a speech from Winston Churchill. The packaging and delivery trucks utilize tongue-in-cheek humor, and customers love posting funny photos of themselves online, decked out in Moosejaw gear. At the time I joined the company, the stores were modeled to be more of a traditional retail experience. We wanted to create a store that was designed to be more interactive, cultivating the fun of the online culture, and a place where customers wanted to come and hang out.

By pulling on the ideas and input from the team, we created stores with lots of interaction—plasma televisions live streaming content, ping-pong tournaments in the stores, Nerf gun battles between employees and customers, and odd promotions like in-store pull up contests that would get you a discount for hitting a certain number. At the time I was forty-six years old and most of the employees were in their early twenties. I brought sensibility and stability to the team, they brought quirky creativity, innovation, and ideas in touch with what our customers most liked. Together we found a way to practically use their humor and zest for living a certain lifestyle to create a strategic business advantage. It took teamwork.

Good leaders know how to get the best out of the people for which they are accountable to lead. They understand each team member is a valued contributor, an important ingredient in the recipe. A leader free from self-interest and not full of ego can pull people together. That leader's desire to be part of something greater is contagious, and others are inspired to be part of that team. A weak leader will try to suppress great ideas and unique abilities from within the team for fear of looking replaceable, but a strong leader is secure in their leadership and understands that facilitating the best efforts of each member creates the greatest outcomes.

> GOOD LEADERS KNOW HOW TO GET THE BEST OUT OF THE PEOPLE FOR WHICH THEY ARE ACCOUNTABLE TO LEAD

Many a leadership book will tell you that when it comes to organizational development, the smartest leaders surround themselves with even smarter people. It is never one person, it is always a group of people. In this, "there is no 'I' in TEAM" has never resounded more loudly. The most effective leaders gather a diverse group of people and form them into a cohesive unit; a team that acts as one—one unified front, one voice, one view—and all the result of honoring diversity and encouraging debate, having discussions, and exploring insights. The "one" emerges from the collective voice of the many, led by a leader who leverages each individual's gifts and perspectives to shape the view. As a team the intellect of the group is leveraged to define the strategy, establish the priorities, determine the tactics and agendas to accomplish the goals and create the outcomes. Lastly, the team measures their progress, their KPIs (Key Performance Indicators), and the milestones which guide them along the way and serve to focus the broader organization. They act as a team. Individual contributions are multiplied through the power of team. The whole becomes greater than the sum of its parts—synergy.

Leading a team requires understanding both intellectually and intuitively where you add value and where you have to respect, appreciate, and allow other elements of the team to emerge. There are areas where their abilities are so much better than your own, where their perspective and experience create tremendous advantage. It is a balancing act between understanding your abilities and the abilities of your team. In the case of Moosejaw, the heartbeat of the team was largely driven by the people who lived and breathed that culture. As the leader I came from the outside. I was new, different, and not like all the others. I did certain things, but I never drove the culture—I rode the wave. I gratefully mined the talent of the team. I appreciated their abilities and acknowledged their contributions. One of my most important jobs was not to get in the way of such immense talent, but to channel it.

Try whistling a symphony. It can't be done. The only way for a composer's vision to be heard as it was meant to be is to harness the amazing talent of each member of the orchestra responding to the conductor in time and from the same sheet of music, playing brilliantly together. Every voice is an important element, but the joy of playing is multiplied by each member performing in harmony alongside others. All have passion, but each brings a different skill. The leader of the orchestra leverages their individual abilities, focusing them to perform together. As each distinctive talent is submitted to the magnificence of achieving something greater together, the result is powerful.

# TEAM CULTURE

A team culture thrives on the collective energy of individuals who are working together as a unit. Babe Ruth was baseball's first member in the Hall of Fame. He was arguably one of the greatest baseball players of all time, but he knew one guy playing great did not win games. Sure, he swung for the fences every time he was at bat, but that was because he had the full support of his team, as they had full support from him. Ruth said, "The way a team plays as a whole determines its success. You may have the greatest bunch of individual stars in the world, but if they don't play together, the club won't be worth a dime." The same could be said of any business organization.

Synergy causes the level of performance of each individual to rise when working together as a team. A high-performance team is never an accident, they are built carefully by a thoughtful leader. It may begin with great talent, but there must also be shared vision and goals. There must be trustworthy behavior and respect among members. Celebration of individual contributions as well as team successes is an important element. When the collective talent and energy is focused and harnessed by an effective leader, the team's potential is unlimited, capable of great things.

Shortly after taking over the chief executive role at Microsoft in 2014, Satya Nadella explained, "The thing I was most focused on early on was, how am I maximizing the effectiveness of the leadership team, and what am I doing to nurture it? Are we able to authentically communicate, and are we able to build on each person's capabilities to benefit our organization?"[4] Good leaders nurture team culture. What an organization stands for and how these things are demonstrated daily is set by the leader through their actions and expectations. The behavior of the team and its teammates is a reflection on their leader. When teammates are inspired to be the best they can be, when they are held accountable to the standards of a thriving, wholesome culture, then the organization as a whole (as well as the individuals within it) prospers.

# BUILDING BETTER TEAMS

If you desire to become a better leader, build a better team. Ask yourself these important questions:

- Do you relish the opportunity to interact with members of your team?

- Your team has much to offer, how can you unlock their potential?

- How can you best leverage their intellect?

- How can you better harness their collective skills and experience?

- Are you creating opportunities for members to contribute to the team in meaningful ways?

- Do they feel valued by you?

- Do you praise them and offer encouragement?

- In what ways do you offer guidance for your team along the path toward the vision?

- Do you know what motivates them?

- What is it that creates enthusiasm in the people you lead?

In all the elements discussed thus far: communication, setbacks, optimism, values, re-framing, accomplishment, curiosity, humility, tenacity, diversity, adventure, and action, we have been weaving a thread throughout the entire book that has led us to this moment. In light of all we have learned, we now consider our ability to lead a team.

Leadership cannot be limited to one attribute, and this book highlights but a few that my experience has shown to be important in the development of a leader. Leadership begins first with leading yourself—intentionally working toward becoming the best you can be. From there it extends out to leading others—inspiring and encouraging them to become the best they can be.

As we move toward a conclusion, we must spend a few moments together talking about legacy. I will share with you the one I am building and hope to leave behind, but the chapter which follows is meant to make you take stock of what is important to you today and think about what might be important to you fifteen or twenty years from now. It is my hope that this book will help you frame and re-frame your concept of leadership until you have clearly in sight what your leadership legacy will look like as it unfolds.

## ENDNOTES

1. *Baboon Fact File* (with permission from African Wildlife Foundation). © Paul Janssen. http://www.outtoafrica.nl/animals/ engbaboon.html. Retrieved from the web on 09/24/18.

2. Ibid.

3. *Primate Sociality and Social Systems* by Larissa Swedell (Queens College, City University of New York/ New York Consortium in Evolutionary Primatology). © 2012 Nature Education. Knowledge Project. https:// www.nature.com/scitable/knowledge/library/primate-sociality- and-social-systems-58068905. Retrieved from the web 09/24/18.

4. *The Four XFactors of Exceptional Leaders* by David Reimer, Adam Bryant, and Harry Feurstein. © 20108 Columbia Business School. Article posted on 09/11/18. https://www.strategy-business.com/article/The-Four-X- Factors-of-Exceptional-Leaders?gko=5222d&utm_source=itw&utm_ medium=20180913&utm_campaign=resp. Retrieved from the web 09/24/18.

**IN A TEAM, YOU BELONG TO SOMETHING GREATER THAN YOURSELF AND LEADING THEM IS AN INCREDIBLE PRIVILEGE**

Chapter Fifteen

# LEGACY
## MAKING A POSITIVE, LASTING DIFFERENCE WITH INTENT

"All good men and women must take responsibility
to create legacies that will take the next
generation to a level we could only imagine."

**JIM ROHN**
Entrepreneur, Business Philosopher

Legacy, what is it? How do you define it? Is legacy what I accomplish? Is it what I leave behind? Is it when the day is done and my life is complete, what my eulogy will say? Is that what legacy is?

Or, is it what my kids will think of me when I am gone? Is legacy the impact I have created while living and the impression I will leave behind when I depart? Will this—my legacy—be something I am proud of?

I don't believe my legacy can be summarized by any single event, but rather through the totality of who Harvey Kanter has been as a person—a husband and father, leader and friend. When I think about legacy, I ask myself how my life's journey will deliver the deeper level of contentment I seek?

My original plan was to wait and not write this conclusion until I had completed all the prior chapters. And by complete I mean all chapters written, edited and distributed, feedback received, chapters rewritten, and the manuscript compiled. I wanted to reserve sharing my thoughts on legacy until I was sure the overarching message of this book was clear. I wanted to tie it all up in a nice, neat bow, incorporating all the main elements discussed and reflecting on all the experiences I shared and stories I told to summarize and define the "greater than" theme. Let's be honest, I was hoping to say something profound here. After all, a conclusion that ends in legacy should be impressive, shouldn't it?

In reality, I have landed on something that is almost a one-liner; something I could have said from the onset. Legacy is not about being heroic. It isn't being a hero, or some larger-than-life figure. Legacy isn't something as tangible as having a star on the Hollywood Walk of Fame. Legacy isn't having a bronze statue somewhere to commemorate my life. Of course, it can be these things, but these things are more symbols of legacy, a representation. Perhaps these things indicate greatness, maybe they say I'm a G.O.A.T. (Greatest of All Time), but I know that's not true. For me legacy is something far simpler. My definition for legacy is closely aligned with my definition for leadership. **I define legacy as having guided and counseled well, having instilled confidence and enthusiasm, having created momentum and been an inspiration to others in their desire to be the best they can be.** If I have managed these things, then my legacy is exactly as I long for it to be.

Put even more simply, I define legacy as making a difference and impacting people in a positive and lasting way. This has been the bedrock of my leadership. It is the cornerstone of my outlook on life.

A leader defines, communicates, and leads by example. Among other core traits of great leadership is their impact on a team, as seen and experienced by their behavior as a team and as teammates. What an organization stands for and how this is demonstrated each and every day is influenced by the leader. That difference is demonstrated by measuring if the impact has been positive and is lasting. Leaders make a difference with intent. They create a positive impact, legacy that lasts, some may call this legacy.

It is fitting to me that my "big finale" is straightforward—simple and clear. The legacy I want to leave is to have made a difference by being here. I hope to have impacted people positively through my relationships with them or their experiences with me. For me, this begins at home with my wife and kids. If the impact I had on them yesterday, have on them today, and will have on them tomorrow and beyond helps them to be better people, to do good, and to live a life that makes a positive difference, then I will have a legacy of which I am proud.

## THE CIRCLE OF LIFE

It just extends from there. If the personal circles I travel in socially and my friends are impacted positively through their relationships with me or, at a minimum, their experiences with me, then I have done well. The circle grows outward regarding my work, my career, and my involvement in my community. If in these areas I can also look back and believe that through a relationship or experience with me I have helped to create a more positive outcome for others, then in my eyes (and hopefully in the eyes of others) I will have done well. I will have left a lasting legacy.

Everything else is just stuff, and hopefully good stuff. Core skills and attributes, the way I do things, the way I communicate, how I share, my orientation around culture, decision making, action and accountability, my involvement with teams, my stories, experiences, and examples are all ways I have tried to communicate leading among others. But when the day is done, leading is creating impact with intent. **Leading is making a positive difference for those you guide and counsel. It is instilling confidence and enthusiasm in them. It is creating momentum and**

**inspiring them in their desire to be the best they can be.** If it seems rather circular at this point, perhaps that's because it is. Making a positive impact with intent through relationships to create outcomes is just another way to define leadership—and I did not need to review all the chapters to bring this point home.

"It is immensely moving when a mature man—no matter old or young in years—is aware of the responsibility for the consequences of his conduct and feels such responsibility with heart and soul. He then acts by following an ethic of responsibility and somewhere he reaches the point where he says: 'Here I stand; I can do no other.'"[1] I believe I have reached that point in my life. What seems to resonate so unequivocally with me today is delivering on what I have been blessed with, and in so doing, helping others to do the same. Each day I seek to do good, to make a positive impact, and to achieve some level of legacy for accomplishing this through people's relationships and experiences with me.

*They do not display themselves;*
*Therefore they are illuminated.*
*They do not define themselves;*
*Therefore they are distinguished.*
*They do not boast;*
*Therefore they advance.*

—Tao Te Ching

**My conclusion is this: to lead well and leave a legacy is to guide and counsel, to instill confidence and enthusiasm, to create momentum and inspiration for others in their desire to be the best they can be**

**... and to do this in a way that makes a positive difference and a lasting impact.**

# YOUR TURN

I pray you never have cancer, or that your mother doesn't lose a leg. It is unlikely you will attend a Jesuit university, and only a handful of you will have the opportunity to climb Mt. Rainier. These experiences are part of what has shaped me. They have framed and re-framed my perspective on leadership. What experiences are shaping yours?

Imagine, if you will, that you are the CEO of digitally-driven company. Your sales are completely dependent upon e-commerce. Let's say you are hit with a DOS (denial of service) attack. A rogue, unidentified hacker has pointed a mal-ware scheme at your company's website which loads it with ten times the normal traffic. This implodes the server and locks your site down. The site crashes and customers cannot browse or purchase anything; you are at a complete standstill.

But wait, it gets even worse. The attack comes late in the fourth quarter at a time when a day's worth of sales is equal to a week, and a week's worth of sales is equal to a month in other quarters.

The hacker holds you up for a ransom. The hacker's identity is completely concealed, but he makes you the offer to cease the cyber attack if you pay 10 bitcoins ($3800/ea., so $38k). He threatens that if you attempt to trace him, he will unleash another mal-ware attack. If you attempt to contact the authorities, he will continue to barrage you and strangle your company's profits. He tells you if you fulfill payment, the attack ceases and he promises not to execute another one.

This is not a scenario you have been trained for. There were no courses that covered how to anticipate or respond to this situation. No business can be done because consumers cannot access the site and each minute down is costing hundreds of thousands of dollars. You know the earnings of the entire year is dependent upon zero downtime. Even the thought of an hour down, let alone the whole site being taken from your control, is the most unnerving challenge you could possibly face in your retail career.

How do you respond? How will you lead in this crisis? The entire team is taking their cues from you. What will your communication with them be? With the hacker? How will the resilience you have developed from previous setbacks serve you in this hour? Will you collaborate with your team or take the reigns and steer the ship?

With no previous personal experience with this scenario, and precious little precedence to draw from because this is a modern attack based on emerging technology and driven at a pace too fast to study, how will your True North hold you? What experiences will you draw from? Whose example will you follow? What is in your gut that reassures you that you are equal to this challenge and confident to stand at the helm and lead the way through?

The kind of leader you are shows up in adversity. It is when things go wrong that you can genuinely assess what leadership attributes have become second-nature and which ones need more development.

In the grand scheme of things, it isn't attributes that will define your leadership, but results. You have read my definition of leadership, and I have shared real-world examples of how this has been formulated, tested, and fleshed out. I have just presented you with a real-world scenario. Put yourself into that situation and think about how you would answer the challenge. Take a thoughtful assessment of yourself as a leader. What kind of leader are you, and what kind of leader do you wish to become? Thinking through how you would handle difficult scenarios before they happen has merit. You have the luxury of making decisions and reflecting on the potential outcomes without the pressure of actual consequences. Test yourself often. In a time of crisis, your leadership "muscle memory" will serve you well.

I invite you to define what "the best you can be" looks like to you and then pursue that for the rest of your life. If you are intentional about how and why you lead, then your legacy will take care of itself. As our time together draws to a close, I want to share this thought with you:

"If you would not be forgotten,
as soon as you are dead and rotten,
either write things worth reading,
or do things worth writing."

**BENJAMIN FRANKLIN**
Founding Father, Author, Printer, Political Theorist, Postmaster,
Scientist, Inventor, Civic Activist, Humorist, and Diplomat

## ENDNOTE

1. Max Weber, German Sociologist and Political Economist known for his thesis of the "Protestant ethic" relating Protestantism to capitalism. https://www. britannica.com/biography/Max-Weber-German-sociologist. Retrieved 10/15/18.

When we met in college, I was known for always asking questions. One of the best I ever came up with was, "Will you marry me?" Robin must have thought I might go places because she said, "Yes!"

Talk about DNA! My daughter, Alex, is a sixth generation retailer, merchant, and leader at Zulily®, the second fastest U.S. e-commerce retailer to reach $1 billion. It's in our blood!

My greatest legacy is defined by my family—the kids I have raised and the family I have today. These I have guided and counseled, instilled confidence and enthusiasm, and hopefully, inspired them to make an impact and leave the world a better place because they were here. My legacy is these people and those whom they touch.

Appendix

# REFLECTION
## HOW I HAVE LED AND WHAT I HAVE LEARNED

"The outcomes of reflection may include a
new way of doing something, the clarification
of an issue, the development of a skill or the
resolution of a problem. A new cognitive map
may emerge, or a new set of ideas may be
identified. The changes may be quite small
or they may be large. They could involve the
development of perspectives on experience or
changes in behavior. The synthesis, validation,
and appropriation of knowledge are outcomes
as well as being part of the reflective process."

**DAVID BOUD, ROSEMARY KEOGH, DAVID WALKER**
Editors of Reflection: Turning Experience Into Learning

As I neared the finish line in completing this book, I sent the manuscript to several peers for their feedback and review. Since author is not a line item on any job description found on my resume, sharing a rough draft of my book with people whom I respect gave me that familiar feeling of being comfortable being uncomfortable all over again. A new adventure. A new experience. A new risk worth undertaking because I believe writing is the next step for me in leading well and leaving a legacy.

The comments I received were thoughtful and offered helpful critiques for improvement. One of those comments suggested I share a glossary of statements, "nuggets of wisdom," that surfaced throughout the book which represent a summary of my reflections across the years on how I have led and what I have learned. These thoughts follow. I trust that the outcome of my reflections may spark in you a new way of doing something, provide clarification of an issue, spark the inspiration to develop a skill or resolve a problem. In all I have shared, it is my hope that you have gained confidence in yourself as a leader and have renewed momentum in becoming the best you can be.

# HARVEY KANTER ON LEADERSHIP

**The job of a leader is to guide and counsel, to instill confidence and enthusiasm, to create momentum and inspiration for others in their desire to be the best they can be.**

---

**A leader makes a positive difference and has a lasting impact.**

---

Leaders have a constant dedication to improvement
and, therefore, develop a life-long orientation to
learning. "You don't know what you don't know."

_____

Leaders engage in adventurous activities which
creates change agility and stimulates the subconscious
to see things from a new point of view.

_____

Leaders must be willing to put themselves into uncomfortable,
vulnerable positions—be comfortable being uncomfortable.

_____

The only given is that whatever you expect to happen is not
going to happen as you expect. Your ability to learn through
the unexpected will grow your leadership capacity.

_____

Leaders are decisive. Many people have trouble making
decisions. Making a decision inherently involves
risk, not making a decision can be even riskier.

_____

How you say something is every bit as
important as what you are saying.

———————————————

"Doing what needs to be done" defines leadership by
actions, not words. A leader willing to act fosters action in
their team and sets the pace for the whole organization.

———————————————

If a problem can't be solved within the frame it was
conceived, the solution lies in re-framing the problem.

———————————————

Passion expressed has an infectious energy.
Leaders who authentically enjoy who they are and
what they do inspire those around them.

———————————————

Leaders communicate clearly, consistently, and often.

———————————————

**A leader's job is not to get people to do things
for their benefit, but to do things for benefit of
those they lead. Leaders serve the people.**

_____

**Setbacks provide you the chance to persevere. When you develop
resilience—the ability to bounce back after a setback—you
increase your capacity to navigate the challenges leaders face.**

_____

**If you don't believe, why should anyone else?**

_____

**Honoring diversity is not about satisfying a quota for gender or
race, it is about understanding the value of bringing together
people from many different backgrounds and experiences
to improve the conversation and explore possibilities.**

_____

**Wherever you lead, your values lead you.**

_____

**A leader's communication is often a balancing act of what vs. why.**

---

**A company's culture is the bedrock of its foundation. Regardless of how great individuals within an organization may be, a healthy cultural environment does not happen without focused intention. Commitment to the defined culture is the way work gets done and how goals get met.**

---

**Leaders focus on the development of people. Then they concentrate on developing their potential to become a model for others.**

---

**Get your ass out of bed and go do what you need to do!**

---

**Tell them again ... and then again. *"Repetitio est mater studiorum,"* or "repetition is the mother of all learning."**

---

Instead of going for a homerun you first go for the single.
Just get on base. You have to be on base to score.
You have to score to win.

---

In business, not taking risks
may be the riskiest thing you could do.

---

Teamwork harnesses the power of
multiplication and creates leverage.

---

Leaders lead. Regardless of position, title, or level of
authority, when you inspire and empower others to
pursue work together as a team, you are a leader.

---

# LEADERSHIP

to guide and counsel,
to instill confidence and enthusiasm,
to create momentum and inspiration for others
in their desire to be the best they can be
... and to do this in a way that makes
a positive difference and a lasting impact!

CHOOSING TO LEAD REQUIRES
# BEING COMFORTABLE
# BEING UNCOMFORTABLE

HARVEYKANTER.COM